Fruits Basket™

Table of Contents

Tohru Honda

The ever-optimistic hero of our story. Recently orphaned, Tohru has taken up residence in Shigure Sohma's house, along with Yuki and Kyo. She's the only person outside of the Sohma family who knows about their Zodiac curse.

Yuki Sohma

At school he's known as Prince Charming. Polite and soft-spoken, he's the polar opposite of Kyo. Yuki is possessed by the spirit of the Rat.

Kyo Sohma

Just as the Cat of legend (whose spirit possesses him) was left out of the Zodiac, Kyo is ostracized by the Sohma family. He greatest wish in life is to defeat Yuki in battle and win his rightful place in the zodiac.

Fruits Basket™

Volume 2

Natsuki Takaya

Translators - Alethea Nibley and Athena Nibley
Associate Editor - Kelly Sue DeConnick
Copy Editor - Carol Fox, Kathy Schilling
Retouch and Lettering - Yoohae Yang
Cover Designer - Aaron Suhr
Graphic Designer - Deron Bennett

Editor - Jake Forbes
Digital Imaging Manager - Chris Buford
Pre-Press Manager - Antonio DePietro
Production Managers - Jennifer Miller, Mutsumi Miyazaki
Art Director - Matt Alford
Managing Editor - Jill Freshney
VP of Production - Ron Klamert
President & C.O.O. - John Parker
Publisher & C.E.O. - Stuart Levy

E-mail: info@TOKYOPOP.com
Come visit us online at www.TOKYOPOP.com

A  Manga

TOKYOPOP Inc.
5900 Wilshire Blvd. Suite 2000
Los Angeles, CA 90036

Fruits Basket Vol. 2

ISBN: 1-59182-604-7

First TOKYOPOP printing: April 2004

20 19 18 17 16 15 14

Printed in the USA

Fruits Basket Characters

Shigure Sohma

The enigmatic Shigure keeps a house outside of the Sohma estate where he lives with Yuki, Kyo and Tohru. He may act perverted at times, but he has a good heart. His Zodiac spirit is the Dog.

Kagura Sohma

Stubborn and jealous as her zodiac symbol, the boar, Kagura is determined to marry Kyo...even if she kills him in the process.

Hanajima & Arisa

The two best friends a girl could hope for. They always look out for Tohru, but they don't know about her new living arrangements...yet.

STORY SO FAR...

Hello, I'm Tohru Honda and I have come to know a terrible secret. After the death of my mother, I was living by myself in a tent, when the Sohma family took me in. I soon learned that the Sohma family lives with a curse! Each family member is possessed by the vengeful spirit of an animal from the Chinese Zodiac. Whenever one of them becomes weak or is hugged by a member of the opposite sex, they change into their Zodiac animal!

Fruits Basket™

Omake Theater: That's right. Hana-chan is an older sister.

HANAJIMA-SAN, I HEAR YOU HAVE A LITTLE BROTHER.
IS HE CUTE?
DOES HE LOOK LIKE YOU? DOES HE?!
...NOT AT ALL.

SEE...?

...WE'RE *NOTHING* ALIKE.

BUT...
...YOU LOOK EXACTLY THE SAME.
I GET THE FEELING... THEY'RE EVEN MORE ALIKE THAN THEY LOOK.
Pay no heed to the aura behind us in the picture.
It's nothing to worry about.

And so...
...a new banquet begins.
AAAHH!

ULTRA SPECIAL BLAH BLAH BLAH 1

I get a lot of letters from people asking me to teach them how to play Dai Hinmin. The way I learned was by playing the video game Sakura Wars 2! (ha ha) But the rules I learned were Sakura rules, so I don't think they're the actual rules. Maybe they're regional rules, or something like that. Like how in Final Fantasy VIII, the card game rules change in each city you visit.

HONDA-SAN!
ARE YOU OKAY?!
YES... BUT SHIGURE-SAN'S BOOKS...
I TOLD YOU YOU DIDN'T HAVE TO HELP.
SHE'S ONLY MOVING THOSE BOOKS...
...SO WE CAN TURN SHIGURE'S LIBRARY INTO *YOUR* ROOM.
I DIDN'T ASK FOR HER HELP.
DAMN RAT!
PERHAPS IF YOU'D JUST DIE, YOU'D BE REINCARNATED AS SOMETHING MORE PLEASANT.
Ah!
YOU'RE THE ONE WITH THE MESSED UP PERSONALITY, DAMMIT!
Um...
HELLO. I'M TOHRU HONDA.

HEY, YOU TWO!
IF YOU HAVE TIME TO FIGHT, YOU'RE NOT WORKING HARD ENOUGH!
I'M A PERMANENT GUEST IN THE SOHMA HOUSEHOLD.
This stack is lighter.
SHIGURE-SAN, SOHMA-KUN...
...KYO-KUN AND I ALL LIVE HERE TOGETHER.
Damn Yuki. Damn Yuki.
MEMBERS OF THE SOHMA FAMILY SHARE A TERRIBLE SECRET.
THEY ARE POSSESSED BY THE SPIRITS OF THE CHINESE ZODIAC.
THIS STRANGE CONDITION CAUSES THEM TO TRANSFORM INTO AN ANIMAL WHEN THEY'RE HUGGED BY A MEMBER OF THE OPPOSITE SEX.

Take that! Moron.
I PROMISED THEM I WOULDN'T TELL ANYONE. OF COURSE, I WOULD NEVER DO ANYTHING TO BETRAY THEIR TRUST!
KYO-KUN, YOU'RE DAMAGING THE BOOKS!
LOOK AT THAT! I FILLED A SHELF FASTER THAN YOU!
Anyway...
THEIR SECRET DOESN'T CHANGE THE FACT THAT THEY ARE KIND AND PLEASANT PEOPLE.
AH.
THEY'RE HERE!
TODAY...
...WE'RE HAVING VISITORS!
I'M REALLY LOOKING FORWARD TO...
...FINDING OUT WHAT KIND OF FUN THINGS WILL HAPPEN NEXT!
DING DONG
WELCOME! DID YOU FIND THE HOUSE ALL RIGHT?!
LET ME...
...INTRODUCE YOU ALL AGAIN!

THIS IS ARISA UOTANI-SAN AND SAKI HANAJIMA-SAN.
THEY'RE MY BEST FRIENDS!
'SUP?
HELLO ...
......
HELLO-- ♡
WELL THEN.
WHY ARE UO-CHAN AND HANA-CHAN HERE?
IT ALL STARTED THREE DAYS AGO...
Begin Flashback
Oi-nk
...WHEN I ASKED IF I COULD TELL THE TWO OF THEM WHERE I WAS STAYING.
HMM...
I DON'T MIND, JUST AS LONG AS YOU DON'T TELL THEM ABOUT THE ZODIAC SPIRITS.

Ah!
THANK YOU SO MUCH!
I CAN'T WAIT TO SEE WHAT KIND OF GIRLS THESE FRIENDS OF YOURS ARE!
SHIGURE-SAN'S FACE DROPPED A BIT...
A YANKEE THUG AND A PSYCHIC FREAK.
...BUT I THINK HE WAS OKAY AFTER I EXPLAINED.
What?!
SO LET ME GET THIS STRAIGHT.
YOU WERE LIVING IN A TENT IN THE WOODS, BUT NOW YOU'RE LIVING WITH PRINCE CHARMING AND ANGER MANAGEMENT BOY? SERIOUSLY?!
YES... I'M SORRY I DIDN'T TELL YOU UNTIL NOW.
IT WAS KIND OF COMPLICATED, BUT NOW EVERYTHING IS FINE!
THEY'RE GOOD PEOPLE. PLEASE DON'T WORRY ABOUT ME.

......

IT'S A BIT OF A SHOCK, THAT'S ALL.

I THOUGHT...

...YOU'D BEEN SPENDING A LOT OF TIME WITH PRINCE CHARMING AND ORANGEY.

...NOW I GET IT.

I WONDER WHAT WOULD HAPPEN IF THE YUKI SOHMA FANS WERE TO FIND OUT...?

......

YOU *REALIZE* WE'RE GOING TO HAVE TO COME OVER.

EH?
TO MAKE SURE IT'S A SUITABLE ENVIRONMENT FOR YOU.

THAT'S A GREAT IDEA, HANAJIMA!
LET'S GO TODAY!
WAIT...IF WE DROP IN UNANNOUNCED, THEY MIGHT NOT HAVE ANY SNACKS FOR US...
GOOD CALL. I MEAN, WE HAVE TO BE CONSIDERATE.
uh.
uh.

THAT SETTLES IT.
THIS WEEKEND, WE'RE STAYING AT *YOUR* PLACE.
OK...
SO...
...NOW IT'S THE WEEKEND.
End of Flashback
PSST! ARE YOU OUT OF YOUR MIND, SHIGURE?
I DON'T THINK THIS IS A GOOD IDEA. THAT GOTH GIRL SEES *WAVES* OR SOMETHING.
HA HA HA
QUE SERÁ SERÁ. EVERYHING WILL BE FINE. REALLY, KYO, YOU WORRY TOO MUCH.
NO, SHIGURE, YOU REALLY *ARE* OUT OF YOUR MIND.
PLEASE, MAKE YOUR-SELVES AT HOME.
...A DOG.

OVER THERE...
EH?
AH! OH.
YOU'RE RIGHT. *BAD DOG!* YOU CAN'T COME IN HERE!
HEY, YOU'RE...
...SHIGURE-SAN, RIGHT? WHAT DO YOU DO FOR A LIVING?
OH, ME?
I WRITE... I'M A NOVELIST.
YOU'RE A NOVELIST?!
WHY ARE YOU SO SURPRISED?!
YOU NEVER ASKED, DID YOU?

WHAT WAS IT? BELLES LETTRES?
I HAD no idea.
Now that I think of it, he is home during the week...
YUP. THAT'S RIGHT.
I WRITE THESE.
Oops!
OH, I'M SORRY. WRONG ONE.
THIS. THIS IS THE REAL ONE!
心悸
HEARTTHROB by SHIGURE SOHMA
SUMMER-COLORED SIGH
THIS IS A BOOK I PUT OUT ON A LARK.
花白ノベルズ
夏色の吐息 1
DOESN'T THAT STILL MEAN YOU WROTE IT?!
THAT'S AMAZING!
WHAT'S SO AMAZING ABOUT BEING A PERV?
FOR ONCE, I AGREE WITH YOU.
*Book: "We can't go back to that summer, but we can always remember...A naughty love story unfolds."

Impressed
TO THINK I'VE BEEN THIS CLOSE TO A NOVELIST...!
HONDA-SAN... YOU'D BETTER STOP OR HE'LL GET A SWELLED HEAD.
DOESN'T SHIGURE ALREADY *HAVE* A SWELLED HEAD?
I MADE ANOTHER NEW DISCOVERY.
THAT MAKES ME HAPPY!
OH YEAH!
I JUST THOUGHT OF SOMETHING REALLY FUN!
PLEASE WAIT HERE A MINUTE!
TOHRU?
IF YOU'LL EXCUSE ME, I HAVE WORK TO DO.
YOU KIDS HAVE FUN.

パタン
......
HMPH. THAT TOHRU...
LOOKS LIKE SHE'S PRETTY USED TO LIVING HERE.
I'M GLAD... AND I UNDERSTAND WHY SHE WAS WORRIED ABOUT TELLING US...
...BUT...
...WE SWORE ON KYOKO-SAN'S GRAVE...
...THAT WE WOULD LOOK OUT FOR TOHRU.
MAYBE THAT WOULDN'T BE A BIG DEAL TO SOME PEOPLE...
...BUT TOHRU WAS OUR FIRST FRIEND.
WE *LOVE* HER.

THERE HAVE BEEN PLENTY OF TIMES WHEN SHE STUCK UP FOR US.
SO THIS TIME... NOT HAVING THE CHANCE TO RETURN THE FAVOR...
...IT'S A BIG DEAL TO US.
WE DIDN'T KNOW...
TOHRU WAS SUF-FERING ALL BY HERSELF.
HMPH. SOME FRIENDS *WE* ARE. WE REALLY LET HER DOWN.
......
SHE WOULDN'T WORRY ABOUT STUFF LIKE THAT.

Summer-Colored Si
HONDA-SAN...
...ISN'T THE TYPE TO SEE HER LIFE...
...AS A GLASS HALF EMPTY.
HUH?
SORRY FOR THE WAIT!
LET'S GET STARTED!
DAI HIN-MIN!

Fruits Basket 2 Part 1:

Nice to meet you and hello. This is Takaya. This is volume 2 of Fruits Basket. It's Prince Charming this time (ha!). This is a bit sudden, but how does everyone shorten the title? Furuba? Furubasu? FB? ...I like "FB"; it's kind of like FF (Final Fantasy!) And Furuba makes me think "Furuba=furui basho," which means "old town" and Furubasu makes me think "Furubasu=furui basu,"which means "old bus" (ha!)! Let's agree to shorten it as Furuba. Now, please enjoy volume 2 of Furuba (ha ha)!

OH.
OKAY...
YES, YES.
FINE, I'LL GO OVER THERE SOMETIME TOMORROW.
YES...
ぎゃあぎゃあ
EH? OH.
TOHRU'S FRIENDS ARE VISITING.
SOUNDS LIKE THEY'RE HAVING FUN.
You bastard! Why don't I teach you a lesson?
I'd like to see you try, bitch!
I have a winning hand.
I knew you'd be good at this.

I ENDED UP LOSING. AGAIN.
ACK...
MY THROAT HURTS FROM YELLING SO MUCH...
STILL, YOU HAVE A NICE BED...
SHIGURE-SAN BOUGHT IT FOR ME.
HE'S ACTING LIKE AN OLD MAN WITH HIS FIRST GRANDKID...
Foosh
Click
HUH? TOHRU...
YOU STILL HAVE THIS HAT?
YES. IT HAS SENTI-MENTAL VALUE.
REALLY? HOW COME?

THAT'S RIGHT. I HAVEN'T TOLD YOU ABOUT IT, HAVE I?
WHEN I WAS STILL SIX OR SEVEN, THE BOYS ALWAYS TEASED ME.
ONE DAY, SOME BOYS WERE CHASING ME AND I WAS REALLY SCARED.
I KEPT RUNNING AWAY AND GOT LOST.
BUT I WAS SCARED OF THE BOYS FINDING ME, SO I HID.
I STAYED THERE ALL NIGHT...
...CRYING AND CRYING.
IN THE MORNING, A BOY APPEARED IN FRONT OF ME WEARING THIS HAT.
HE STARED AT ME FOR A WHILE, AND THEN RAN OFF.
I COULDN'T HELP MYSELF-- I JUST *HAD* TO FOLLOW HIM.

PLEASE WAIT.
PLEASE DON'T LEAVE.
I WANT TO GO HOME!
AH!
OH, NO! I CAN'T CATCH UP ...
......
SEVERAL TIMES...
...I THOUGHT I HAD LOST HIM.

BUT EACH TIME...
...HE WOULD WAIT FOR ME.
huff
huff
wheeze
はっ
HE WAS A MYSTERIOUS BOY.
......
I WENT TO THANK HIM, BUT I COULDN'T FIND HIM ANYWHERE.
THE ONLY PROOF THAT HE WAS EVER THERE AT ALL WAS THE HAT HE GAVE ME.
THEN I REALIZED...
...THAT HE HAD LED ME *HOME.*

Ha Ha!
I'LL NEVER SEE HIM AGAIN.
WHAT A WONDERFUL MEMORY.
IT WOULD BE AN EVEN BETTER STORY...
...IF YOU MET HIM AGAIN AND FELL IN *LOVE!*
YOU NEVER KNOW. IT'S A SMALL WORLD.
YOU'RE RIGHT.
WELL, IF I DID MEET HIM, I'D WANT TO THANK HIM.
OF COURSE, BY NOW...
...HE'S PROBABLY FORGOTTEN ALL ABOUT IT.
How to Grow Delicious Vegetables

......
YOU POOR GIRL.
YOU'VE HAD A TOUGH TIME EVER SINCE YOU WERE LITTLE, HUH?
SIGH... IN A WAY...
THAT BOY...
...WAS MY FIRST LOVE.
THAT'S NOT TRUE AT ALL!
I'M ALWAYS BEING REMINDED...
...OF HOW LUCKY I'VE BEEN.
I GET TO LIVE WITH THE SOHMAS...
...I HAD A MOTHER WHO LOVED ME VERY MUCH...

...AND I HAVE...
...THE TWO BEST FRIENDS IN THE WORLD...
...HANA-CHAN AND UO-CHAN...
...WHO ARE ALWAYS THERE FOR ME.
YOU TWO...
...HAVE BEEN SUCH A SUPPORT TO ME.
I LOVE MY LIFE....

THEY UNDERSTAND.
EH?
YES...
...AND I LOVE YOU BOTH.
...TOHRU-KUN *IS* THAT KIND OF PERSON.
"SHE WOULDN'T SEE IT THAT WAY."
THE KIND WHO FOCUSES ON WHAT SHE **HAS**...
....
"SHE ISN'T THE TYPE TO SEE HER LIFE...
...AS A GLASS HALF-EMPTY."
...NOT WHAT SHE'S **MISSING**.

AND ONE WHO TREASURES...
...BEING WHERE SHE IS NOW.
WE HAVE AN UNRIVALED FRIEND-SHIP...
DON'T WE?
YUP!
....

HEY, YUKI.
GAH.
YOU...
......
...YOU... THAT IS...
SOHMA-KUN ISN'T A MORNING PERSON, IS HE?
Good morning.
WAKE UP, DAMMIT!
HE'S EVEN *STRONGER* WHEN HE'S SLEEPING.
He's already tried.
BUT I'M IMPRESSED, KYO-KUN.
EVEN THOUGH YOU WANTED TO HIT HIM, YOU WOULDN'T ATTACK SOHMA-KUN IN HIS SLEEP!
THAT'S NOT QUITE IT...

AND THAT MEANS HE'S ALWAYS GOING *EASY* ON ME.
HE'S **THICK-SKINNED** AND **COLD-HEARTED.**
HE DOESN'T EVEN HAVE TO TRY!
I HATE THAT DAMN RA--
ダダダダダ
HEY! WEREN'T YOU ASLEEP?!
YOUR STUPID VOICE WOKE ME UP.
FINE, DAMMIT. SEE IF I CARE! BUT I'M TAKING YOU DOWN ONE OF THESE DAYS, YOU HEAR ME?!
Trash can
WHAT ARE YOU BABBLING ABOUT THIS EARLY IN THE MORNING?
I WON'T STOP UNTIL I DEFEAT YOU!

A cat and a mouse ...
THAT'S WHAT THEY'RE LIKE.
See? They're always fighting. Wasn't there a cartoon like that...?
Tom and Jerry?
OH YEAH... THEY'RE HERE.
You two really don't get along, do you?
Yeah, well...
STILL, IT SEEMS LIKE THIS HOUSE IS PRETTY FUN.
IF ANYONE HAD HURT TOHRU-KUN...
...I was thinking of all the things I would do to them...Yes, all of them...
WHAT THINGS...?
BUT...

...YOU TWO...
YOUR WAVES ARE *DIFFERENT*, BUT THEY ARE *GOOD* WAVES...
HUH...?
OH, YOU DIDN'T REALIZE? THAT'S GOOD, TOO...
WELL...
ALL RIGHT, BOYS. WE'RE COUNTING ON YOU TO TAKE CARE OF ONE THING AND ONE THING ONLY--
OUR LITTLE TOHRU-KUN.
UO-CHAN, HANA-CHAN...
じ〜
Whatever, just put down the trash can.
IT'S LIKE THEY'RE GIVING HER AWAY TO BE ***MARRIED***...

Now let's get breakfast.
Yes, breakfast.
WE'LL COME BY AGAIN SOON.
YES...I'D LIKE TO FURTHER INVESTIGATE THE STRANGE WAVES COMING FROM THE SOHMA HOUSE.
HEY HEY HEY!
I DON'T KNOW ABOUT HAVING WOMEN OVER SO MUCH...
OH, I PROMISE I'LL BE VERY CAREFUL WITH YOUR SECRET!
UO-CHAN AND HANA-CHAN ARE REALLY...
...SO, UM...
...REALLY GOOD PEOPLE. SO...
DAMMIT ...
JUST DO WHAT YOU WANT.
THEY'RE YOUR FRIENDS, HONDA-SAN.

...SINCE TOHRU-KUN CAME...
...YUKI AND KYO HAVE MATURED.
I WOULD LIKE TO SEE THEM CONTINUE IN THAT DIRECTION.
OF COURSE, KNOWING YOU, YOU PROBABLY THINK THE WHOLE PLAN'S DOOMED TO FAIL.
It's the beginning of the banquet.
Wherever the journey might lead...
Where's Shigure?
I think he went out.

I FEEL SORRY FOR YOU...
TOHRU-KUN IS A DOZEN TIMES A BETTER PERSON THAN YOU ARE.
......
I AM WELL AWARE OF WHEN MY GLASS IS HALF EMPTY.
Whether good or ill will come of this venture...
...even God doesn't know.

Chapter 8

IT'S ALMOST TIME FOR THE CULTURAL FESTIVAL!
CULTURE FEST
ONLY 6 MORE DAYS
Focus on teamwork, everyone!
This way, this way.
AH HA HA
EVERYONE IS SO EXCITED!

ESPECIALLY MY CLASS, 1-D.
WE'VE PASSED ALL THE SANITATION INSPECTIONS...
...SO WE HAVE PERMISSION FROM THE FACULTY TO SELL ONIGIRI AT THE FESTIVAL.
NOW WE MUST DECIDE WHAT FLAVORS OF ONIGIRI TO MAKE.

ULTRA SPECIAL BLAH BLAH BLAH 2

If you'd like to know what Momiji is saying in German, he says, "What a surprise! How lucky!" "Nice to meet you," "I'm so happy to meet you," and "You're so cute!". This will all make sense shortly! (Ha ha!)

ONIGIRI...
IT ALMOST FEELS LIKE DESTINY.
I know!
WHY DON'T WE HAVE THREE-FLAVORED ONIGIRI?!
I LIKE THAT. IT'S CUTE.
IT'S FUN TO HAVE THREE TASTES IN ONE ONIGIRI.
Ehhh?!
WE SHOULDN'T DO THAT, SOHMA-KUUUUN.
WHAT WOULD HAPPEN IF SOMEONE GOT CHICKEN, KELP, AND PLUM?
EW. THAT'S DISGUSTING!

WHAT'S REALLY DISGUSTING IS YOUR BLATANT JEALOUSY.
SHE BROUGHT AN IRON PIPE TO SCHOOL!
It's got bloodstains on it!
HOW ABOUT WE HAVE BATTLE ONIGIRI?
BATTLE?!
A ONE-ON-ONE MATCH.
WEAPONS ARE ALLOWED, BUT NO KILLING...
...DELIBERATE BLOOD-SPILLING OR TRYING TO CUT OFF SOMEONE'S ARM.
NO.
DEFENDING HONOR AND YOUR RIGHT TO EAT ONIGIRI IN ONE GLORIOUS FIGHT!

Fruits Basket 2 Part 2:

I'll start from the beginning. This is the story of a video game. That's right, Final Fantasy 8. This has spoilers in it, so if you are in the middle the game or plan on playing it, I recommend that you not read this. Okay? Here I go. Let's go back one game first. I played FF7, and beat it normally. (Oy.) I think, somehow, it was special. I've been playing FF since number 4, but the first time I broke down crying was 7. I had never cried about a game before. It still makes me cry. Whenever I hear Aeris's theme, I cry. And of course I think it's stupid to keep crying, but still. Such sadness and pain and helplessness—why couldn't I have done more? To be continued...

DON'T POUT, KYON-KYON.
I HAVE TO GO TO A STUDENT COUNCIL MEETING.
WILL YOU DECIDE WHO BRINGS WHAT?
DON'T CALL ME KYON-KYON!
SURE! LEAVE IT TO ME! ♡
WAIT! THERE'S SOMETHING I WANT TO ASK YOU.
YUKI, RIGHT HERE...
YEAH, YEAH.
YUKI-KUN, I HAVE A QUESTION!
AAAA AHH!
CATS!
EEP!
What's wrong, meow?
meow
WHAT THE?!
Why are you angry, meow?
A fight?
meow
meow
meow
meow
WHAT?!
How...?
From there.

KYO...
KYO-KUN...?!
I DON'T CARE ANYMORE!
WAIT, KYON-KYON! WHAT'S WITH THE CATS?!
Don't break the door down!
...WHAT WAS THAT?
Yay!
Kitties!
I HAVE NO IDEA.
WHAT ATTRACTED THE CATS?
sigh
That's strange...
EEP!
DON'T WORRY ABOUT IT. YOU'RE PRETTY STRANGE YOURSELF.
INDEED. HE ACTS LIKE A BAD LITTLE BOY.
STILL, HE REALLY DOES HAVE A TEMPER, DOESN'T HE?

"I'VE ALWAYS WISHED...
...THAT I COULD BE LIKE THAT."
SO...
...SOHMA-KUN IS JEALOUS OF KYO-KUN...
EVEN THOUGH THEY HAVE SO MUCH RESPECT FOR EACH OTHER'S QUALITIES...
...THEY CAN'T GET ALONG.
...AND KYO-KUN IS JEALOUS OF SOHMA-KUN?

BUT IF YOU ASK ME...
...THEY EACH HAVE THEIR OWN WONDERFUL QUALITIES.
SO WHY...?
ACK!
Uuhh...
WALKING AND THINKING AT THE SAME TIME IS DANGEROUS...
hee
hee hee
Pff
hee hee
hee

Someone saw me....
Oh...!
GOOD EVE...NING...
......?
I WONDER WHO THIS IS...?
WHY IS THERE A BOY...
...IN THIS BUILDING SO LATE AT NIGHT?
What an outfit...
1-D 42 Tohru Honda
TOHRU?
EH?!
TOHRU HONDA?!
AH, UM, Y-YES, THAT'S... RIGHT?
Sieh do!!
Welch ein Glück!!

!! A FOREIGNER?
Ich freue mich, Sie zu seheh!
Sehr Angenehm!!
UH...
UM, I'M SORRY, I DON'T SPEAK YOUR LANGUAGE...
I told you there'd be German!
Sehr hübsch!
!!
UH--
UM--
WAH--
EX--

EXCUSE ME!
HONDA-SAN...? WHAT'S THE MATTER?
A--
huff
huff
wheeze
A WEIRD F-FOR-FOR--!
A WEIRD FORK?
Came to pick her up
......
IT WAS A WEIRD FOREIGNER!
HE SURPRISED ME. HE... KISSED ME!
......
WH-WHO WAS HE...?
HONDA-SAN.

DID SOMETHING HAPPEN?
DID SOMEONE... HARASS YOU?
HUH?! NO...!
I DON'T WANT HIM TO WORRY...
I-
I'M SORRY. IT WAS NOTHING.
UM... THANK YOU FOR ALWAYS COMING TO PICK ME UP.
DON'T WORRY ABOUT IT...
IF THERE'S ANYTHING TROUBLING YOU...
...YOU CAN TELL ME ABOUT IT.
I'LL HELP YOU.
AH...!
THANK YOU VERY MUCH...

SOHMA-KUN IS SO KIND.
AND SO IS...
...KYO-KUN.
WHY MUST THEY...
...ENVY EACH OTHER AND FIGHT?
WHY CAN'T THEY SEE...
...THEIR OWN WONDERFUL QUALITIES?
KAIBARA Public High School
CULTURE FEST
Everyone come!
......
Flyer

Fest...?

WHAT THE HELL?

ARE YOU PLANNING TO OPEN AN *ONIGIRI SHOP* OR SOMETHING?

NOT REALLY... IT'S NORMAL FOR ME.

AH! GOOD MORNING!

YOU'RE ALWAYS UP EARLY.

Ah!

KYO-KUN, THAT'S--!

--A LEEK ONIGIRI.
WHY WOULD YOU MAKE SOMETHING LIKE THAT?!
ER...UM... IT'S FOR THE FESTIVAL.
I WAS DOING RESEARCH FOR THE SURPRISE ONIGIRI...
I'll eat them myself when I'm done.
KYO-KUN, DO YOU HAVE ANY SUGGESTIONS?
SALMON AND COD ROE ARE ALL THAT BELONG IN ONIGIRI!
I'LL JUST MAKE MY OWN.
!!
KYO-KUN! YOU'RE REALLY GOOD AT MAKING ONIGIRI!
THAT'S GREAT! I NEVER WOULD HAVE GUESSED!
AH?!

WHEN I WAS TRAINING, I MADE MY OWN MEALS.
BUT MAKING IT LOOK NICE AND HAVING IT TASTE GOOD ARE TWO DIFFERENT THINGS.
IF YOU ASKED SOMEONE WHO WAS TRAINING TO PREPARE ONIGIRI...
...I THINK THEY WOULD BE JEALOUS OF HOW WELL YOU MOLD THEM.
LIKE ANYONE'D TRAIN FOR *THAT*.
Honestly, where do you come up with these things?
...REALLY?
......
Pi.
Good morning, it is now 6:15.
It's a fine winter morning, and...
THAT DOESN'T CHANGE THE FACT THAT IT'S A WONDERFUL THING...
WHY...
...CAN'T HE SEE?
...AH.
MAYBE IT'S STUCK ON HIS BACK...

HUH?
IF YOU THINK OF SOMEONE'S GOOD QUALITIES...
...AS THE *UMEBOSHI* IN AN ONIGIRI...
...IT'S AS IF THEIR QUALITIES ARE STUCK TO THEIR BACK!
PEOPLE AROUND THE WORLD ARE LIKE ONIGIRI.
EVERYONE HAS AN UME-BOSHI WITH A DIFFERENT SHAPE AND COLOR AND FLAVOR.
BUT BECAUSE IT'S STUCK ON THEIR BACK...
...THEY MIGHT NOT BE ABLE TO SEE THEIR UMEBOSHI.
"THERE'S NOTHING SPECIAL ABOUT ME.
I'M JUST WHITE RICE."
THAT'S NOT TRUE.

THERE IS AN UMEBOSHI-- ON YOUR BACK.
MAYBE...
...THE REASON PEOPLE GET JEALOUS OF EACH OTHER...
...IS BECAUSE THEY CAN SEE SO CLEARLY THE UMEBOSHI ON OTHER PEOPLE'S BACKS.
I CAN SEE THEM, TOO.
THERE'S AN AMAZING UMEBOSHI...
I CAN SEE THEM PERFECTLY.
...ON YOUR BACK, KYO-KUN.

SOHMA-KUN IS WONDERFUL.
KYO-KUN...
...IS WONDERFUL, TOO.
...!
TH--
THAT'S *EXACTLY* WHAT I'M TALKING ABOUT! WHERE DO YOU COME UP WITH THAT STUFF?
AND WHY DOES IT HAVE TO BE AN *UMEBOSHI?* SOME METAPHOR!
I-I'M SORRY. SHOULD I HAVE USED SALMON?
tweee
AH! OH, THE KETTLE...
....
...HEY.

YOU KNOW...
...THERE'S ONE ON YOUR BACK TOO.
I CAN SEE IT.
AN UMEBOSHI.
EVEN NOW...
...SOMEONE MIGHT BE ENVYING ANOTHER...
...FOR SOMETHING THEY DON'T SEE IN THEM-SELVES.
Really? Really?!
It's a little plum.
A reeeeeally tiny one.
I love little plums!
THEY MIGHT BE LONGING FOR A QUALITY THEY ALREADY POSSESS.

WHEN I THINK OF IT THAT WAY...

...EVEN JUST A LITTLE...

...I REALIZE THAT I NEED TO DO MY BEST WITH THE QUALITIES I HAVE, EVEN IF I CAN'T ALWAYS SEE WHAT THEY ARE.

...HEY.
THE FRAME IS SHAKY.

HEY, IT'S NOT LIKE WE'RE BUILDING A HOUSE, CAT-LOVER.
YEAH, CAT-LOVER.
IT'S FINE AS LONG AS IT DOESN'T BREAK, CAT-LOVER.

WHY THE HELL DO YOU KEEP CALLING ME CAT-LOVER?!
Are you making fun of me?!
OH, WE KNOW.
YOU TALK TOUGH, BUT UNDERNEATH, YOU'RE A NICE GUY WHO LOVES ANIMALS.

WHEW... HIS SECRET'S SAFE!
HE COMES BACK AND IT GETS ALL NOISY.
WITH HIS PERSONALITY, I'D LOVE TO SEE HIM CUT LOOSE AT A PARTY.
HE CAME BACK WITHOUT MUCH OF A FIGHT.
THAT'S UNUSUAL...
BECAUSE SOHMA-KUN IS SOHMA-KUN...
...AND KYO-KUN IS KYO-KUN.
IF THIS KEEPS UP, ORANGEY'LL HAVE A FAN CLUB TOO BEFORE LONG.
Haha.
THAT'S VERY POSSIBLE.
HUH?
YU-KI-KUUUUUN. ♡

SENPAI...
ACTUALLY, WE HAVE A PRESENT FOR YOU, YUKI-KUN. ♡
WE ALL PITCHED IN TO BUY THIS, HOPING YOU'D WEAR IT AT THE FESTIVAL. ♡
EH?
TA-DAAAAAH! ♡
A COSTUME ESPECIALLY FOR YUKI-KUN! ♡

NOW IT'S COMING BACK TO ME.

SERIOUSLY.

BECAUSE YOU SHOWED THIS TO HIM.

KAIBARA Public High School
CULTURE FEST
Let's Celebrate
Our Culture
Everyone welco

OH, COME ON! WE'LL GET TO SEE YUKI AND KYO.

YOU HAVEN'T SEEN THEM IN A WHILE EITHER, RIGHT, HA'RI?

AND TOHRU HONDA WILL BE THERE, TOO.

...

I'M SURE YOU'LL LIKE HER, HA'RI!

MOMIJI.

YOU'VE MET TOHRU HONDA?

Ja!
Now...
Sehr hübsch!!
POTATO
Miso Flavor
...how will the Festival turn out?
Wow...
I didn't think he'd like it this much.
Whoa, Sohma, hang in there!
What the...?

Chapter 9

*Sign: Onigiri Shop; The dreaded "Surprise Onigiri"

ULTRA SPECIAL BLAH BLAH BLAH 3

I've wanted to. I've wanted to do this. CROSS-DRESSING!! (ha ha) Until now, I've been drawing stories that don't have any room for it, so with Furuba, I thought, "You will do it, Yuki!" (Mind out of the gutter!) But boys with feminine faces are destined to cross-dress (or be made to)...think...if you asked him, I'm sure he'd hate me for it (ha ha).

Fruits Basket 2, Part 3:

It seemed like that feeling had almost disappeared. FF7 was too special. At least to me. Yes, yes, back to FF8. There are people who thought the Draw system was unending agony, but I enjoyed it. Anyway, if I didn't Draw, I felt unfulfilled. I would keep Drawing and not try to advance the story. Even when I was about to die, I would keep Drawing and Drawing. Oh, that was nice (ha ha). It's fun. Uh-huh, uh-huh. The cards were fun, too. Laguna-san was cute. I liked Irvine, too. Selphie is criminally adorable.... I really love her, Sel-Sel. Sensei enjoys eating monsters like there's no tomorrow (too bad they didn't animate it). The Devour command knocked me out. I love that type of command! And I hate Omega (ha ha)! Why is he hundreds of times harder than the last boss (ha ha)?! I had to keep casting Meltdown to do any damage (ha ha).

......
CAN'T YOU TELL YUKI-KUN DOESN'T LIKE IT?
WELL, YEAH, BUT HE'S...
...TOO CUTE!
YEAH...
SOHMA-KUN IS THE ONE BRINGING IN ALL OUR CUSTOMERS...
THAT'S RIGHT.
Do it for us, in memory of the three years we've spent together at high school!
...IS WEARING GIRL'S CLOTHES TODAY.
SOHMA-KUN, UNABLE TO REFUSE A REQUEST OF THE THIRD-YEAR STUDENTS...
Please please please!
IT'S ALREADY CAUSED AN UPROAR.
EVERYONE HAS BEEN COMING TO OUR CLASS, WANTING TO SEE SOHMA-KUN DRESSED AS A GIRL--GIRLS, BOYS, EVEN TEACHERS.
AS A RESULT, WE'VE BEEN ABLE TO SELL DOZENS OF ONIGIRI.

BUT SOHMA-KUN DOESN'T SEEM TO BE ENJOYING IT.
!
He's sitting in a chair.
AND...
...FOR SOME REASON, I FEEL LIKE...
...HE'S AVOIDING ME.
Even at the house...
I WONDER... IF I UPSET HIM SOMEHOW...
AW, LEAVE HIM ALONE.
HE'S PROBABLY JUST HUMILIATED TO BE DRESSED LIKE A GIRL.

HE'S REALLY SELF-CONSCIOUS...
...ABOUT HIS PRETTY FACE.
REALLY? BUT A LOT OF PEOPLE ARE JEALOUS OF HIS LOOKS.
Is that how it is?
DAMN YUKI. FINALLY GETTING WHAT HE DESERVES!
WHAT...
...SHOULD I DO?
WHEN I SAW HIM DRESSED LIKE THAT...
...I THOUGHT, "OH, HE'S SO CUTE!" BUT...
DON'T WORRY ABOUT IT. MOST PEOPLE THINK SO.
That's right. No matter how you look at him, he makes a pretty girl. Bwa ha ha...
BUT SOHMA-KUN IS REALLY HURT RIGHT NOW...
...AND HE'S STILL DRESSING LIKE A GIRL FOR EVERYONE.
HE'S REALLY...

...VERY KIND.
Du lieber Himmel!!
WHY DOES YUKI LOOKS LIKE A mädchen!
?!
!!
WH-WHAT THE--?
AH...!
THAT'S THE BOY WHO KISSED ME ON THE CHEEK THE OTHER NIGHT!

¥100
WHAT'S *HE* DOING HERE?
!?
EH?!
DON'T WANDER AROUND BY YOURSELF.
Ja!
......!!
MOMIJI.
YOU *KNOW* HIM, KYO-KUN?
HEY.
YOU LOOK WELL, YUKI.
KYO.

HA...
KYAAHH!
SO HANDSOME!
HE'S SO CUTE!
A FRIEND OF YOURS, YUKI-KUN?!
Guten tag!
I'M MOMIJI SOHMA. I'M HALF GERMAN, HALF JAPANESE!
AND THIS IS HATORI SOHMA.
SO CUTE!
WE'RE RELATIVES OF YUKI AND KYO!
!
IS THIS TRUE, KYO-KUN?!
...YEAH.
Hmph...
FORGET ABOUT MOMIJI, WHAT IS *HATORI* DOING HERE?

BUT DOES THAT MEAN...
...THESE TWO ARE ALSO IN THE CHINESE ZODIAC?
THIS IS SUCH A COINCIDENCE!
I MET A SOHMA WITHOUT EVEN KNOWING IT!
IT'S NO WONDER THAT MOMIJI-SAN WAS ALSO SURPRISED!
THAT BEING SAID, YUKI...
...WHEN DID YOU BECOME A WOMAN?
HOW DARE YOU SAY THAT AFTER YOU'VE SEEN ME NAKED SO MANY TIMES...
EEEEE-HHH?!
WAH! YUKI-KUN, DOES THAT MEAN...
NO! IT CAN'T BE!
Can it?
SOHMA, YOU...!
Are you?!
NO!

NOW, TAKE A DEEP BREATH.
......
HE'S MY DOCTOR...
These clothes. How do you take them off?
YOU DON'T HAVE TO EXAMINE ME *HERE*...
I'm both relieved and disappointed!
Ooooohhh.
WELL, I WOULDN'T *HAVE* TO IF YOU'D JUST COME TO YOUR MONTHLY CHECK-UP LIKE YOU PROMISED.
SOHMA-KUN...! ARE YOU SICK?
EH... OH, NO.
YUKI HAS WEAK BRONCHIAL TUBES.
It should get better as he gets older. This is merely preventative.
WHEN HE WAS LITTLE, HE'D HAVE ATTACKS ALL THE TIME.
......!
YOU'RE TOHRU HONDA-KUN?
AH...YES. NICE TO MEET YOU.

...I SEE.
?
YOU REALLY *ARE* A "NORMAL" GIRL.
HATORI ...
HEY!
DON'T CLIMB ON THE BOOTH!
Was?
WHAT ARE YOU DOING, YOU IDIOT?!
MOMIJI .....
Don't walk on it!
OH NO!
I-I'LL BE RIGHT BACK...!
......
I told you!
I said don't move! Argh.
IF YOU'VE GOT A PROBLEM WITH IT, TELL MOMIJI. HE'S THE ONE WHO BROUGHT ME THE FLYER.
WHY DID YOU COME HERE?

WHEN AKITO SAW IT, HE SAID *HE* WAS GOING TO COME, TOO.

WHA?!

HE HAD A FEVER OF 102, THOUGH, SO AS HIS DOCTOR I PUT A STOP TO IT.

BUT I HAD TO COME IN HIS PLACE...

...AS MOMIJI'S CHAPERONE.

YOU'RE NOT DOING A VERY GOOD JOB.

Argh! What's going on?!

Just get over here, moron!

I WOULD RATHER HAVE COME SOME EVENING WHEN THERE WEREN'T SO MANY PEOPLE AROUND.

......

DON'T WORRY.

I DIDN'T COME HERE TO DO ANYTHING TO TOHRU HONDA.

AKITO IS THE ONE WHO MAKES THAT DECISION.

HOWEVER, I WILL SAY THIS--

YOU WON'T GET VERY FAR IF YOU TRY TO THREATEN ME IN *THAT* OUTFIT.

And why are you the only one cross-dressing?

THANK YOU. SO MUCH.

ALL RIGHT, NOW YOU'RE GOING TO STAY HERE AND BE QUIET!

Or go home!

KYO HIT ME!

WAAAAAAA!

K-KYO-KUN...

AH!

TOHRU! IT'S TOHRU!

HOW ARE YOU, HOW ARE YOU? I CAME HERE TO SEE YOU!

Where were you?

HELLO... YOU'RE FROM THE SOHMA FAMILY, RIGHT?

Um, well, I've been here for a while...

Ja!

WE HAD A FATEFUL ENCOUNTER BEFORE!

YOU'VE MET BEFORE...?

WE MET AT PAPA'S BUILDING!

Uh.

Uh.

PAPA'S THE MANAGER OF THAT BUILDING, SO I PLAY THERE A LOT!

Ehhh?!
REALLY ?!
HEY...
I've been cleaning a Sohma building this whole time?!
HEE, TOHRU'S SO DUMB!
And Sohma-kun never said anything when he came to pick me up!
But...but the building's name is different...!
HEY, HEY, TOHRU!
*Yuki didn't know either.
YOU KNOW ABOUT THE ZODIAC THING, RIGHT!
UH, YES.
THEN I CAN HUG YOU!
Yay!
HOLD IT, LOVER-BOY.
HE SAID, "I CAN HUG YOU." THAT MEANS--!
But she won't mind if I transform, right?
That's not the problem! Think of where we are!
HE REALLY IS ONE OF THE CHINESE ZODIAC!
Eke!!
ARE YOU HOGGING TOHRU BECAUSE SHE'S SO CUTE?!
I BET KYO HUGS HER EVERY DAY!

YOU STU--!
WHO WOULD WANT TO--!
MY TURN! ♡
AH!
!!
WH- WHAT WAS *THAT?!*
AN EXPLOSION ?!
TOHRU?!
HEY, WHAT HAPPENED?
......

......
This bright pink thing.
Hey!
THESE ARE MOMIJI-KUN'S CLOTHES!
EH? NO WAY. WHAT HAPPENED?! DID HE EXPLODE?!
Ah... Uhh... umm...
EH?
......
HUH? WHAT'S WITH THE RABBIT?
WHERE'S MOMIJI-KUN?!
THIS IS TERRIBLE!
THAT'S WEIRD. WHY WOULD MOMIJI JUST TAKE OFF HIS CLOTHES AND WANDER AWAY?
AND THAT RABBIT... WHERE DID IT COME FROM?
Something strange is going on...
WHAT HAPPENED, TOHRU?!
IT'S TOO WEIRD. SAY SOMETHING, HONDA-SAN!
WEIRD?

IN THAT CASE, I TOO...
...AM WEIRD.
BECAUSE HERE I AM DRESSED LIKE THIS, AND YOU'RE ALL GOING ON ABOUT RABBITS.
IT MUST NOT SUIT ME AFTER ALL...
You idiot!
YOU'RE THE BEST, SOHMA!
YOU'RE SO LOVELY!
He's right! You look incredible!
If you were really a girl, we wouldn't leave you alone!
No matter how I look at you, all I see is woman!
Believe in yourself!
...thanks.
Thank you, Sohma-kun.
YOU DIVERTED THE CONVERSATION, USING YOURSELF AS A SACRIFICE...!
DAMN IDIOT! DOES HE EVEN KNOW WHAT HE'S DOING?!
HE WON'T BE ABLE TO HOLD HIS HEAD UP FOR A WEEK.

BUT, BUT--!
THEY'RE *SCARY*, TOHRUUU.
Don't go crying to her!
SO YOU'RE THE RABBIT...
And I see that you're a boy, as well.
SERIOUSLY, YOU'RE LUCKY YUKI THREW THEM OFF.

Hmph.
HE'S ALWAYS TRYING TO STEAL THE SPOTLIGHT WITH HIS LOOKS.
I DON'T CARE WHAT HE SAYS, I THINK YUKI *LIKES*--

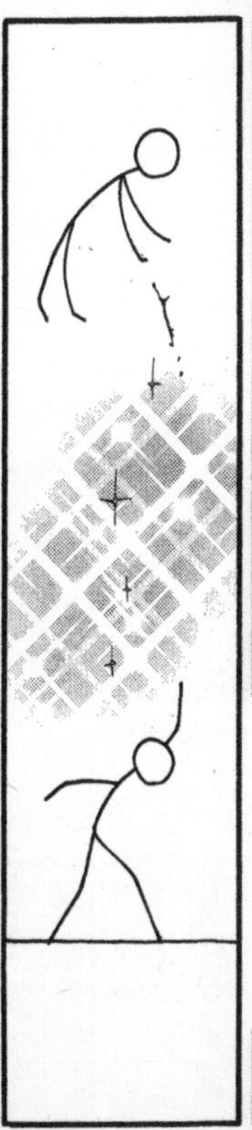

WANT ME TO SEND YOU HIGHER...?
DAMN RAT...

MOMIJI, YOU HAVE TO BE CAREFUL.
YOU NEED TO THINK ABOUT *REPERCUSSIONS,* MOMIJI.
NOW, WE HAD BEST BE GOING.

OOOOH... SO *SOON?!* BUT I STILL WANNA TALK TO *TOHRU!*
I DON'T MIND IF YOU STAY...

YOU PROMISED THAT IF THERE WAS A PROBLEM...
...YOU'D COME HOME IMMEDIATELY!
Go home!
H-Ha'ri, you're boring...

OH...I ALMOST FORGOT SOMETHING IMPORTANT.
YUKI, KYO. LINE UP OVER THERE.
Just do it.
HUH?
WHAT?

I WANT A CONCISE ANSWER.
WHAT IS TWO PLUS ONE?

AKITO TOLD ME TO TAKE A PICTURE OF YOU TWO.

THREE?

HAAATORII!
THIS IS A GREAT PORTRAIT.
LATER.
Bis bald!

Wait, dammit! Gimme that cameraaaaa...!
I DIDN'T...
...FIND OUT ANYTHING ABOUT HATORI-SAN.
Maybe he isn't one of the Zodiac?

MY LIFE IS OVER...

WHAT WILL AKITO SAY...

...WHEN HE SEES ME IN THIS OUTFIT?

......

Somehow, it's not funny anymore.

Kyaaaaahh!

SOHMA-KUN, YOU'LL CATCH COLD!

YOUR TRACTOR-- I MEAN, TRACHEA...!

IT'S HARDER TO ENDURE WEARING THIS OUTFIT...
My trachea will be fine.
B-BUT EVERYONE WAS SO HAPPY.
GUYS DON'T LIKE BEING CALLED *CUTE*...

......

I'M SORRY. I'M AS GUILTY AS EVERYONE ELSE. I THOUGHT YOU WERE CUTE, TOO.

......

I DIDN'T WANT YOU TO SEE ME EITHER, HONDA-SAN.
IN THIS RIDICULOUS--
I LOOK LIKE AN *IDIOT*.

I REALLY SHOULD HAVE TOLD THEM NO.
BECAUSE IT MEANT...
...SHE WAS SAYING, "I LOVE YOU SO MUCH!"
Tohru, you're so cute!
squeeze
UH, UM, BUT I...
...I WAS SO HAPPY WHEN MOM TOLD ME I WAS CUTE.
IT MADE ME HAPPY.
WORDS...
...OF LOVE.
MOM...
MOM...
...I WON'T EVER...

...HEAR HER SAY THAT AGAIN.
SO EVERYONE IS SAYING THAT THEY LIKE YOU, SOHMA-KUN...
Um, uh, you see?
I-I KNOW IT PROBABLY SOUNDS LIKE I'M JUST TRYING TO RATIONALIZE IT...
...AND I KNOW I'M NOT REALLY MAKING SENSE...

NO...
...IT'S STRANGE. I DON'T MIND SO MUCH WHEN YOU SAY IT, HONDA-SAN.

...COULD YOU HELP ME OUT WITH THIS?

THIS DRESS IS SO COMPLICATED! IT'S AS HARD TO TAKE OFF AS IT IS TO PUT ON.

Chuckle
WELL, MAYBE I'LL KEEP UP THE FAN SERVICE A LITTLE LONGER. FOR THE SAKE OF THE ONIGIRI SALES...
BUT BEFORE THAT...

My hair is caught on a button.

I THINK IT WOULD LOOK GOOD ON YOU, HONDA-SAN.

NO, I COULDN'T. BUT IT'S BEAUTIFUL. IT'S LIKE A PRINCESS DRESS.

Ah ha ha!

YOU'RE CUTE.
ON YOU, HONDA-SAN ...
...I'M SURE...
...IT WOULD BE VERY PRETTY.

……
THANK YOU.

SHOULD WE GO BACK TO THE CLASSROOM?

UH...

うあああ
Oh no!
I-I DON'T KNOW WHAT TO SAY! I DON'T KNOW WHETHER TO FEEL SHOCKED, MOVED, FLATTERED OR UPSET!
I DON'T KNOW WHAT'S GOING ON, BUT I CAN'T BELIEVE SOHMA-KUN THINKS I'M CUTE!

THAT'S RIGHT.

Oh my!
Oh my!

MORE THAN BEING "CUTE," OR "PRETTY"...

...SOHMA-KUN IS...

...A REAL "PRINCE CHARMING."

Did you get the camera back?
Shut up! No!

Ah.

OH YEAH. HONDA-SAN.

Y-YES?!

I KNOW THIS MIGHT SOUND ODD, BUT... IT'S ABOUT HATORI.

EH?! HOW COME?

IF YOU EVER MEET HIM AGAIN, TRY NOT TO BE LEFT ALONE WITH HIM.

WELL...

HATORI HIMSELF ISN'T ALL BAD.

....

BUT REMEMBER THE INCIDENT I TOLD YOU ABOUT, WHEN MY SECRET WAS DISCOVERED?

THE ONE WHO SUPPRESSED ALL OF THEIR MEMORIES...

...WAS HATORI.

!

I WAS A LITTLE WORRIED... I THOUGHT I SHOULD TELL YOU.

♪ピーン・ポーン・パーン♫

Paging Tohru Honda-san from class 1-D, Tohru Honda-san from class 1-D...

Please come to the conference room on the first floor immediately.

I repeat, Tohru Honda-san from class 1-D...
EH?
I WONDER WHAT IT IS...?
EH?! ME?!
UM, I-I'LL BE RIGHT BACK!
'Kay.
"THE ONE WHO SUPPRESSED ALL THEIR MEMORIES"...
I NEVER THOUGHT THE DAY WOULD COME WHEN I'D ACTUALLY MEET SOMEONE WHO COULD DO SUCH A THING.
HELLO.
I'M SORRY FOR CALLING YOU HERE LIKE THIS.
KYO SEEMED TO HAVE HIS HANDS FULL, BUT WITH YUKI THERE, I DIDN'T THINK I'D GET A CHANCE TO SPEAK TO YOU IN PRIVATE.
RIGHT AFTER I WAS WARNED, HERE I AM, **ALONE** WITH HIM!
HERE'S MY ADDRESS.
COME VISIT ME ON YOUR NEXT DAY OFF.
EH?!

I WOULD LIKE TO TALK TO YOU AT LENGTH...
...ABOUT SOMETHING IMPORTANT.
PLEASE DON'T MENTION IT TO YUKI OR KYO.
I THINK YOU KNOW WHAT THIS IS ABOUT.
THE ONE WHO SUP-PRESSED ALL THEIR MEMORIES WAS HATORI,
SUPPRESSED
SUPPRESSED
SUPPRESSE
SUPPRESS
UPPRESS
SUPPRE
SUPPR
THEIR MEMORIES
UPPRE
SUPPRESSE
PRESSED
UPPRE
THEI
EMOR
THEIR
MEMORIES
SUPPRES
THEIR
MEMORIE
SUPPR
THE
WH--
WHAT SHOULD I DO? IF I SAY NO, WILL HE SUPPRESS MY MEMORIES ANYWAY?
B-BUT IT MIGHT BE SOME-THING REALLY IMPORTANT.
THAT'S RIGHT. MOM SAID I SHOULDN'T BE TOO MISTRUSTING!
...O
OKAY!
EXCELLENT.
YOU MIGHT EVEN GET TO MEET AKITO, AS WELL.
EH?!

ドキッ
Keine Sorge!
(Don't worry.)
I'LL BE THERE TO MAKE SURE HA'RI DOESN'T DO ANYTHING DIRTY!
SO COME ON, TOHRU!
LOOK, YOU...
TOHRU IS A MÄDCHEN. SHE'D BE SCARED TO BE LEFT ALONE WITH A MAN.
ドキ ドキ
H-HE'S BEEN LISTENING?
BUT IF MOMIJI-SAN WILL BE THERE, THEN I FEEL A LITTLE BETTER...
A SURPRISE SUMMONS FROM HATORI-SAN...
I WONDER WHAT HE WANTS TO TALK TO ME ABOUT?

Chapter 10

ULTRA SPECIAL BLAH BLAH BLAH 4

Hatori stands out so much that I originally thought he would be on the cover of volume 2....his personality makes him easy to draw. I feel like he and Shigure are popular as a set. I wonder how Hatori feels about that (laugh).

IT JUST GOES TO SHOW HOW MUCH A PART OF THIS HOUSE TOHRU-KUN HAS BECOME.
SHUT UP! IT'S *HER* FAULT FOR NOT GOING OUT MORE OFTEN.
WHERE IS THE FLOWER OF OUR HUMBLE HOME?
WHAT WAS THAT?
WHAT ARE YOU, STUPID?
草摩
*Sohma
WOW...
IT'S SO GRAND...

AS HATORI-SAN INSTRUCTED...
...I CAME WITHOUT TELLING SOHMA-KUN AND THE OTHERS.
TH-THE SOHMAS REALLY ARE AN IMPORTANT FAMILY.
BUT TO THINK I MIGHT MEET AKITO-SAN, THE HEAD OF THE FAMILY...
Hallo!
TOHRU!
Eh..
KYAAAH!
MO-MOMI-LOO-LOOK OU-L-LOOK O--
YOU'RE RIGHT ON TIME!
COME ON IN!

カラ カラ…
Excuse... me...
WELCOME ...
...TO THE SOHMA ESTATE!
Ha'ri lives over here.
WOW...
EVEN THE GROUNDS ARE HUGE.
IT'S LIKE ITS OWN LITTLE TOWN.
BUT IT'S VERY QUIET.
AS IF NO ONE LIVES HERE...
BUT THIS ATMOSPHERE...
...IT CERTAINLY ISN'T EASY ON MY NERVES!
Ha'ri's house is separate from the main house!

WAS IT THAT LONG A TREK?
She's tired from nerves.
N-NO...
I'M GLAD YOU'RE HERE.
H-HELLO. UM... I'M SORRY... I DIDN'T BRING ANYTHING...!
DON'T WORRY ABOUT IT.
MOMIJI, GET US SOMETHING TO DRINK.
Ja!
SIT WHEREVER YOU LIKE.

THERE'S A PICTURE...
HATORI-SAN'S MOTHER...?? PROBABLY NOT...
I WOULDN'T EXPECT HIM TO HAVE A PICTURE OF A WOMAN.
HE SEEMS SO SOLEMN.
FOR SOME REASON, NO MATTER WHAT HE SAYS, HE SOUNDS LIKE HE'S ANGRY.
COULD IT BE THAT THE IMPORTANT THING HE WANTED TO TALK ABOUT WAS... MY INCOMPETENCE?!
はっ
TOHRU ?
TOHRU, ARE YOU SICK? SHOULD WE HAVE HA'RI EXAMINE YOU?
I-I-IT'S ALL RIGHT. I'M FINE!
Nothing a check-up could fix!

HATORI-SAN, YOU'RE A DOCTOR, RIGHT?
DON'T YOU HAVE AN OFFICE AT A HOSPITAL?
AH? OH. I DON'T WORK AT A HOSPITAL.
I'M THE SOHMA FAMILY DOCTOR; I DON'T EXAMINE ANYONE OUTSIDE THE FAMILY.
WELL, HALF OF IT IS TAKING CARE OF AKITO.
YOU COULD SAY HE SPECIALIZES IN GETTING SICK.
HE MUST HAVE A WEAK BODY...
IT'S QUIET, ISN'T IT?
TODAY THE PEOPLE "INSIDE" ARE AT THE INNER GATE, PREPARING FOR THE NEW YEAR'S CELEBRATION.
NEW YEAR'S IS THE BIGGEST EVENT OF THE YEAR!
EVEN "OUTSIDE" PEOPLE HELP. EVERYONE'S REALLY BUSY.

AH.
INSIDE?
OUTSIDE?
Really?!
TH-THAT'S AMAZING...!
IT IS?
Well, it's not exactly common.
REMEMBER THAT TREE-LINED ROAD YOU TOOK TO THE MAIN HOUSE?
ALL THE PEOPLE WHO LIVE ALONG THAT ARE SOHMAS.
THIS IS A WORLD THAT MOST PEOPLE LIKE ME WOULD NEVER SEE...
A-am I out of place?!
Main House (Inside)
(Person)
(Outside)
(Empty can)
Tree-lined road
(Cat)
"OUTSIDE" THERE'S ABOUT EIN HUNDERT... ONE HUNDRED PEOPLE. "INSIDE" THERE SHOULD BE ABOUT FIFTY.
PEOPLE WHO LIVE "INSIDE" ARE PEOPLE LIKE US, AND PEOPLE WHO KNOW OUR SECRET.
SHII-CHAN AND YUKI USED TO LIVE "INSIDE," TOO.
BUT KYO LIVED "OUTSIDE."
Shii-chan is Shigure's nickname.
When you grow up, you can have a house and live outside if you want, like Shii-chan.

TURNING IT AROUND...
...THAT MEANS THERE ARE VERY FEW PEOPLE WHO KNOW ABOUT THE SECRET, EVEN INSIDE THE FAMILY.
IT'S UNTHINKABLE THAT A COMPLETE STRANGER LIKE YOU SHOULD KNOW SUCH A SECRET.
NORMALLY, I WOULD HAVE SUPPRESSED YOUR MEMORIES IMMEDIATELY.
ギキッ
"THE ONE WHO SUPPRESSED THEIR MEMORIES WAS HATORI..."
BUT AKITO DIDN'T GIVE THE ORDER, AND EVEN ALLOWED YOU TO *LIVE* WITH THEM.

I'VE BEEN THINKING ABOUT THAT...
...AND I'VE COME TO A CONCLUSION.
C...CON-CLU-SION?
DO YOU ENJOY LIVING AT SHIGURE'S HOUSE?
YES! VERY MUCH!

I THINK IT BEST...
...YOU LEAVE THAT PLACE.
DO NOT INVOLVE YOURSELF WITH THE SOHMA FAMILY ANY MORE.
OH...
I'M SURE SHIGURE DIDN'T MAKE CLEAR THE GRAVITY OF OUR CONDITION.
THE SOHMA FAMILY CONTINUES TO BE POSSESSED BY VENGEFUL SPIRITS. IT'S NOT THE FUN AND GAMES YOU MIGHT THINK.
IT'S BIZARRE...
SINISTER...
...CURSED.

AKITO IS TRYING TO *USE* YOU.
"CURSED"...
BEFORE YOU REGRET GETTING INVOLVED WITH THE SOHMA...
...GET OUT.
ding dong
ding dong
WAIT HERE.
I'LL JUST BE A MOMENT.
CURSED ...?
WHAT COULD BE SO TERRIBLE ABOUT THEIR SECRET? AND USING ME... FOR WHAT?
I-I DON'T QUITE UNDERSTAND...
HE SAYS I SHOULD LEAVE...
This probably isn't about transforming...
... BUT...

Fruits Basket 2 Part 4:

I got the feeling that the last bosses in FF were getting weak.... Was it my imagination? I don't mind if they're weak! (Because then it's easier.) "End of Heart" gives me chills. While I was playing FF, I was playing Angelique. I like Sei-lan. And I like Oscar. Whenever Rachel starts dating one of them (especially Sei-lan) I reset the game. Even when she starts going after the other boys, I reset (laugh)! You're all like that too, right? I even played the RPG. Arios (cry). I wanted the two of us to be happy together... (What happened to Sei-lan?) And now I'm in the middle of Suikoden 2. Actually, I played 1, and I didn't like it much, but 2 is fun! As expected, I like Jowy...The name of my group is The Natsuki and Jowy Army!

...BUT I...
ABOUT HA'RI...
...HE'S ALMOST BLIND IN HIS LEFT EYE.

HA'RI USED TO HAVE A GIRLFRIEND.
HER NAME WAS KANA. SHE WAS HIS ASSISTANT.
SHE WAS A VERY SWEET PERSON.
EVEN WHEN SHE FOUND OUT HA'RI WAS POSSESSED BY A VENGEFUL SPIRIT, SHE LAUGHED AND SAID SHE DIDN'T CARE.

...
SO HATORI-SAN IS ONE OF THE CHINESE ZODIAC!
THEY WERE ENGAGED TO BE MARRIED.
BUT...
...AKITO GOT MAD.
HE GOT REALLY MAD AND WENT INTO A RAGE. HE WOULDN'T ALLOW THEIR MARRIAGE.
AND HE HURT HA'RI'S EYE.
BUT HA'RI DIDN'T...
...BLAME AKITO.
INSTEAD, KANA BLAMED HERSELF.
SHE KEPT AGONIZING, SAYING IT WAS HER FAULT HA'RI'S EYE GOT HURT.
It would...
EVENTUALLY, SHE GOT HEARTSICK.
...it would have been...
SO...

...been better if...
...HA'RI ERASED KANA'S MEMORIES.
HE COULDN'T WATCH HER FALL APART.
...if we had never met.
SO HE ERASED THE TIME WHEN THEY LOVED EACH OTHER.
KANA LEFT.
POOR HA'RI...
HE CRIED...
...BUT...
...HE DIDN'T BLAME AKITO.
......
WHY...?
IT MUST HAVE BEEN PAINFUL.

BECAUSE THAT...
...IS PART OF THE CURSE.
THAT'S WHY...
...I DON'T KNOW WHAT AKITO IS THINKING...
...BUT I UNDERSTAND A LITTLE OF HOW HA'RI FEELS.
HARI DOESN'T WANT TO SEND TOHRU AWAY LIKE KANA.
HE DOESN'T WANT...
...TOHRU TO BE HURT LIKE KANA WAS.

HUH?
EH?! ARE YOU CRYING?!
WHY?!

DID... DID I MAKE TOHRU CRY...?
SORRY... I'M SORRY.
NO... THAT'S NOT IT.

HATORI-SAN IS...

...TOO KIND A PERSON...

I'M CRYING BECAUSE...

...HE WAS WORRIED ABOUT ME.

EVEN THOUGH HE MIGHT BE THE ONE...

...WHO NEEDS KINDNESS MOST RIGHT NOW.

I'M GLAD...

...I'M JUST SO GLAD...
...I GOT TO MEET EVERYONE.
EVEN IF I AM BEING USED FOR SOME PURPOSE...
...GIVING ME THE LIFE I HAVE NOW...
...I WANT TO SAY THANK YOU.
I WILL NEVER REGRET...
...THAT I GOT INVOLVED.
I NEVER COULD.

I'M THE WAY I AM NOW...
...BECAUSE OF SOHMA-KUN AND THE OTHERS.
WHAT ABOUT ME...?
ARE YOU HAPPY YOU MET ME?
OF COURSE!
...
TOHRU IS LIKE A *MUTTI*-- SHE MAKES ME FEEL SAFE!
Mutti?
IT'S ALL RIGHT.
WE DIDN'T GET YOU INVOLVED WITH OUR MESS...
...INTENDING TO HURT YOU, TOHRU-KUN.
AND WE'RE NOT USING YOU.

Shi-
SHIGURE-SAN?!
Shii-chan!
Guten tag!
ANYWAY, HATORI EXAGGERATES.
And he likes to order people around.
WH-WHY DID YOU COME HERE?

INTUITION! INTUITION, MY DEAR TOHRU-KUN!

STOP LYING. YOU JUST CAME TO SEE HOW PREPARATIONS FOR NEW YEAR'S WERE GOING.

A NOVELIST MUST HAVE A SHARP SIXTH SENSE!

And then to see Akito.

HAA-SAN, IF YOU WORRY TOO MUCH, YOU'LL GO BALD YOU KNOW.

I KEEP TELLING YOU AKITO DOESN'T MEAN ANY HARM, BUT YOU WON'T TRUST ME EVEN A LITTLE.

AND YOU'RE EVEN SCARING TOHRU-KUN... WHAT WOULD YOU DO IF SHE REALLY LEFT?

Average people always envy genius.

Would you just stop living like a jellyfish?

THEY ACT LIKE THAT, BUT THEY REALLY ARE FRIENDS.

......

AH!

UM, I'M... IT'S OK.

THANK YOU SO MUCH FOR WORRYING ABOUT ME.

BUT I STILL WANT TO LIVE THERE...

コツ。

HERE. I'M GIVING THIS TO YOU BEFORE I FORGET.

IT'S THE CAMERA I USED AT THE FESTIVAL.

Eh...

EH?! WHY?!

WHY...?

?

WASN'T THAT THE AGREEMENT?

HE...

THAT IF YOU CAME HERE I WOULD GIVE YOU THE CAMERA?

...HE NEVER SAID THAT!

What's in the camera? Huh? Huh? What is it?

Quiet, you hack.

THEY'RE BOTH SO STUBBORN, THEY'RE ALMOST ALIKE...

ドキッ
OH... YOU STILL HAVEN'T MET AKITO.
AH, IT'S NO GOOD.
I WENT TO SEE HIM EARLIER AND GOT SHOOED AWAY.
I think he's in a bad mood.
Ah,
AAAAAHH! AH! UM!

P-PLEASE, DON'T WORRY ABOUT IT. MORE IMPORTANTLY...
...MORE IMPORTANTLY, HATORI-SAN... YOU'RE ONE OF THE CHINESE ZODIAC, RIGHT?!
WHICH YEAR ARE YOU?!

ぷいっ
ぷい

THAT'S A GREAT QUESTION, TOHRU-KUN!
OH WOW, THIS IS REALLY GOING TO BE GOO--
ーぷ
ーぷ
ーぷ
SHIGURE...

I WILL TELL EVERYONE IN THE PUBLISHING INDUSTRY EVERYTHING I KNOW ABOUT YOU, STARTING FROM WHEN YOU WERE FOUR YEARS OLD...
SORRY, TOHRU-KUN. MY LIPS ARE SEALED!

YOU KNOW SHE'S GOING TO FIND OUT SOMEDAY!

No!

AND *YOU*, STOP ASKING STUPID QUESTIONS!

Y-YES, SIR.

I KEPT MAKING YOU CRY...

W-WAS THERE A FUNNY ZODIAC SIGN?

......

I'M SORRY...

...ABOUT TODAY.

...DIDN'T I?

......
THAT HATORI.
CALLING YOU OUT HERE LIKE THAT AND CAUSING TROUBLE...
...BUT HE'S NOT A BAD GUY, REALLY.
YES...

HE SEEMS LIKE A VERY KIND PERSON.
I...
...CHANGED THE SUBJECT FROM AKITO-SAN...
...EVEN THOUGH HATORI-SAN SEEMED FINE WHEN HE SAID HIS NAME.
"He's almost blind in his left eye."
"He hurt Hari's eye."
"Akito is trying to use you."
DOES HE LIKE HIM?
"Akito-san's word is law."
"I can't go against Akito's decision."
IS HE AFRAID OF HIM?
"THAT IS...
"THAT IS PART OF THE CURSE."

...kun...
TOHRU-KUN!
IF WE GET SEPARATED, YOU'LL GET LOST.
JUST NOW...
JUST NOW, COULD THAT...
TOHRU-KUN?
COULD THAT HAVE BEEN...
A...
SHIGURE... SAN?
WHAT IS...
...THE "CURSE"?

DO I...
DO I HAVE TO DO ANYTHING?
AS FOR THE REST... I THINK IT'S STILL TOO EARLY TO TELL YOU.
I'M SORRY.
YOU ...
...JUST NEED TO BE YOU.
I FEEL LIKE I'VE LEARNED A LOT...
...AND YET, I HAVEN'T LEARNED A THING.
I HAVE A STRANGE FEELING ABOUT TODAY.
THE SOHMA FAMILY.
WILL THE DAY EVER COME WHEN I UNDERSTAND EVERYTHING ABOUT THE SOHMAS, GOOD AND BAD?
THE DAY WHEN...

...I MEET HIM?
...IT'S TRUE.
A *KOTATSU* CAN EVEN PUT LITTLE DEVILS TO SLEEP.
Cheese...
Fish...
Whether they get along or not. These two certainly don't.
Hey you two, wake up.
Don't you want dinner?
EITHER WAY...
WORRYING ABOUT IT WON'T HELP.
WHATEVER WILL BE, WILL BE. WHATEVER WON'T, WON'T. THAT'S LIFE.
Like que será será.
Shigure is rubbing off.
THAT'S RIGHT.
NO MATTER WHAT...

THE WAY I FEEL ABOUT THEM WON'T CHANGE.
AND THE DAYS I LIVE IN THIS HOUSE...
...ARE PRECIOUS...
...PRECIOUS DAYS.
HEY, HEY, LET'S STICK ROOTS UP THEIR NOSES.
ぷぷー
WE...
WE CAN'T! THAT WOULD HURT!
Okay then, leeks.

Omake Theater: This has nothing to do with the manga, but right now I have a fever of 100.4F...

CAN YOU REALLY SEND OUT ELECTRO-MAGNETIC WAVES?
IS IT USEFUL?
LIKE, CAN YOU *KILL* PEOPLE WHO MAKE YOU MAD?
I WOULDN'T DO THAT.

MY CLASSMATE FROM FOURTH GRADE...

...THE KEEPER OF THE CLASS PET...

...I think he's out of the hospital by now.

Chapter 11

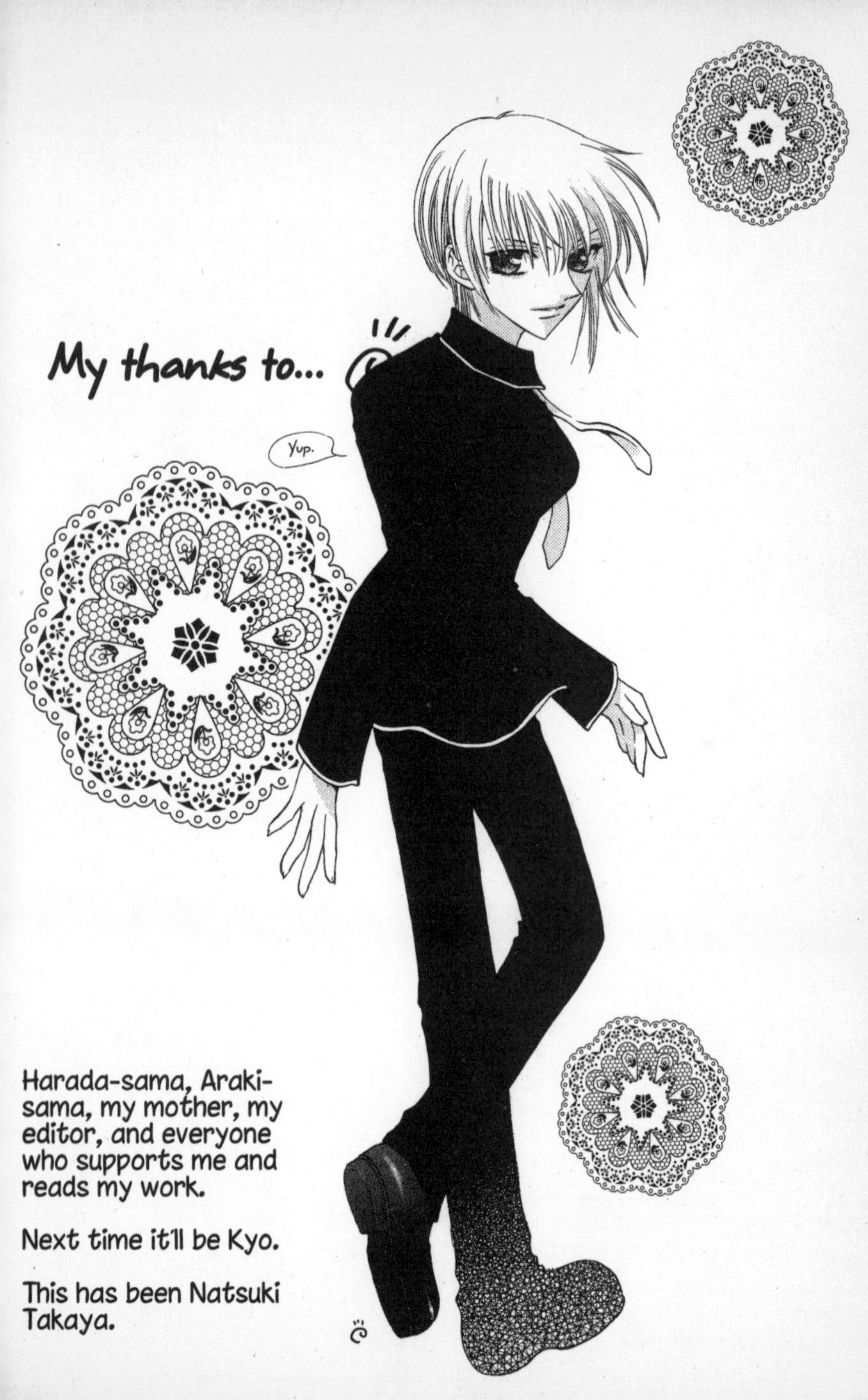
My thanks to...
Yup.
Harada-sama, Araki-sama, my mother, my editor, and everyone who supports me and reads my work.
Next time it'll be Kyo.
This has been Natsuki Takaya.

ULTRA SPECIAL BLAH BLAH BLAH 5

In reality, the costume for the dance of the Chinese Zodiac is different every year. But here I have Momiji and Yuki wearing the same costume because I thought that if they had different costumes, it would be hard to understand. And on a completely different note, my older sister really liked Hana's line, "May you have good waves next year too..." (laugh). By the way, she seems to really like Kyo. She's a cat-lover.

IT'S BEEN FOUR MONTHS SINCE SHE STARTED LIVING WITH US.
BUT THERE'S STILL SOMETHING I HAVEN'T GRASPED.
WE'RE NOT GOING BACK!

YOU THINK SOMEONE WHO LEFT HOME FOUR MONTHS AGO WOULD GO BACK JUST BECAUSE IT'S NEW YEAR'S?!

IF I WENT HOME TO ATTEND A BANQUET, THERE'D BE NO POINT IN HAVING LEFT.

WE'RE NOT GOING BACK!
ポリポリ
DEAR, OH DEAR...
WHAT'S WRONG?

YOU SEEM TO HAVE BEEN ARGUING FOR A WHILE...
LISTEN, TOHRU-KUUUN...
THEY SAY THEY WON'T GO BACK TO THE SOHMA ESTATE FOR NEW YEAR'S!
YOU'RE TOO OLD TO BE TATTLING!
It's pathetic!
I said it. Pyon!
YOU'RE NOT GOING HOME?
BUT MOMIJI-SAN SAID THAT THE NEW YEAR'S FESTIVITIES ARE A MAJOR EVENT FOR THE SOHMA FAMILY.
INDEED. IT'S THE BIGGEST EVENT OF THE YEAR FOR US.
THE *WHOLE FAMILY* COMES HOME AND CELEBRATES.
AND THE MOST IMPORTANT PART IS THE JUUNISHI BANQUET.

THE BANQUET CAN ONLY BE ATTENDED BY THOSE POSSESSED BY THE SPIRITS OF THE CHINESE ZODIAC.
THE ZODIAC MEMBERS REPRESENTING THE NEW YEAR AND THE OLD YEAR DANCE TOGETHER.
THIS YEAR IT WILL BE MOMIJI-KUN AND THE TIGER.
Ooohh!
YUKI'S DANCE THREE YEARS AGO WAS BEAUTIFUL!
Wow!
I WOULD LOVE TO HAVE SEEN THAT!
DON'T TELL HER ABOUT THAT!
... Yes sir.
Pickled radish
IT MUST BE WONDERFUL.
A BANQUET. JUST LIKE THE LEGEND!
HMPH. IT'S GOT NOTHING TO DO WITH ME.
THE *CAT* CAN'T *GO* TO THE BANQUET.

Ehh?!
WHY...?
IT WAS DECIDED LONG AGO THAT THE CAT COULDN'T COME.
I GUESS *THAT'S* JUST LIKE THE LEGEND TOO.

......
BUT...

LOOK, IT'S NO BIG DEAL SO YOU DON'T HAVE TO GO AND MAKE THAT FACE.
I'M NOT SAYING I WON'T GO HOME JUST BECAUSE OF SOME STUPID BANQUET.

IT'S BECAUSE IF HE WENT BACK, *KAGURA* WOULD BE SO MOVED THAT SHE'D *KILL* HIM.
SHUT UP!
......
NEVER MIND THAT.

IF WE GO BACK TO THE SOHMAS, WE'LL HAVE TO SPEND THE THREE DAYS OF SANGA-NICHI* THERE, RIGHT?
DURING THAT TIME, HONDA-SAN WOULD BE LEFT ALL ALONE.

!
HUH? YOU'RE NOT GOING TO YOUR GRANDPA'S HOUSE?

* The first three days of January

Aloha!
Ooooh!
Grand-pa...
TOHRU-KUN'S GRANDFATHER AND THE REST OF THEM ARE GOING TO HAWAII.
SO SHE ASKED ME TO LET HER STAY *HERE* FOR NEW YEAR'S.

WHAT? YOU'RE GOING TO BE ALONE FOR NEW YEAR'S?
THAT'S WHAT I JUST SAID!

SHUT UP! THIS IS THE FIRST TIME I HEARD ABOUT IT!
THAT'S BECAUSE YOU DON'T LISTEN.
Ha ha!
OH, YOU TWO.

THANK YOU FOR THINKING OF ME.
SOMEHOW, THAT...
...FILLS MY HEART...
...WITH JOY!
BUT I'D FEEL TERRIBLE IF YOU MISSED OUT ON SUCH A WONDERFUL CELEBRATION ON MY ACCOUNT.
AND IT'S BEEN A WHILE SINCE YOU'VE SEEN YOUR PARENTS, RIGHT?
I'M SURE THEY'RE ANXIOUS FOR YOU TO COME HOME.
じ ん
PLEASE, GO ENJOY THE NEW YEAR WITH YOUR FAMILY. YOU CAN LEAVE THE HOUSE TO ME WHILE YOU'RE AWAY!
I'LL MAKE SURE TO TAKE...
... GOOD CARE OF--

Oh no!
I LEFT THE BATH WATER RUNNING!
WE TRUST YOU, TOHRU-KUN.
Aaaaah!
...I THINK.
I'M GOING BACK.
WE DON'T REALLY...
...HAVE A CHOICE, DO WE?
NOT WHEN SHE PUTS IT LIKE THAT.
It's been a while since you've seen your parents right?
...BECAUSE SHE'LL NEVER SEE HER OWN...
Thank goodness I made it in time.
SHE KNOWS ...
...WHAT IT MEANS TO LOSE TOUCH WITH PARENTS...
...EVER AGAIN.

Fruits Basket 2 Part 5:

The "Those with Wings" (Takaya-sensei's last manga series before Furuba) CD was released on June 5th. Did you buy it? Did you listen to it? It's a comedy and it's really funny, so I'd really like you to hear it. They got an amazing cast who all did a great job (of course) and I ended up laughing at my own jokes (laugh). When I went to the recording session, I was so nervous I was shaking. I was like, "Wow, the big time!" (laugh). I'm such a fan of Midorikawa-san that my friends often tell me, "We know already; you don't have to say it again," and when a certain anime was on and it turned out that he played the new character, my friend called and said, "You must be really happy, Takaya," and as soon as I got off the phone, I sent out a FAX that said that I really was very happy, but now I'm really, really happy! When I met him I shouted, "I love you! I adore you! I'm a huge fan!" (laugh)

PLEASE BE SAFE.

WATCH OUT FOR CROWDS.

IT'S OKAY. THERE AREN'T MANY PEOPLE OUT NOW.

AND YOU BE CAREFUL TOO, HONDA-SAN. MAKE SURE TO LOCK UP.

I WILL!

HAVE A SAFE TRIP!

I'M SURE...

...SHE'LL BE FINE.

HONDA-SAN *IS* PRETTY CARELESS.
SHE FELL DOWN THE STAIRS AGAIN YESTERDAY.
SHE EVEN WALKS INTO WALLS.
SHE COULD CHOKE ON A GRAIN OF RICE FOR ALL WE KNOW.
....
THAT'S NOT FUNNY.
YOU GUYS.
STOP FUSSING OVER HER LIKE MOTHER HENS.
It's embarrassing to listen to.
HUH?
SHE'LL BE FINE...
THIS ONE TIME...
...SHE LEFT HER WINDOW WIDE OPEN.
DON'T TELL ME YOU WENT IN?
LIKE I'D DO THAT! I SAW IT FROM *OUTSIDE!* SHEESH!

I KNOW YOU'RE WORRIED ABOUT TOHRU-KUN, BUT YOU DECIDED TO COME WITH ME, SO--

I-I'M *NOT* WORRIED!

THIS WORRYING IS STUPID.

LET'S GO.

Ah!

COME TO THINK OF IT...

...THERE *WAS* A REPORT IN THE MORNING NEWS ABOUT A BURGLARY IN OUR NEIGHBORHOOD.

THEY SAY THE ROBBER IS STILL AT LARGE.

Damn!

SHE'S JUST NAÏVE ENOUGH TO INVITE A BURGLAR INSIDE!

SHE'D PROBABLY SERVE HIM TEA AND ASK HIM QUESTIONS ABOUT HIMSELF!

Aaaaaah!

Interesting.

NOW, NOW, YOU TWO...

IF YOU KEEP STANDING THERE IN A DAZE...

Look what they're saying about you, Tohru.

... Someone will crash into you.

WAH!

W...
WELL, IF IT ISN'T SAKI-CHAN.
Why can't she appear like a normal person?!
What's with the cape?
MY, THIS IS A COINCIDENCE. WE WERE JUST ON OUR WAY TO OUR FAMILY'S ESTATE.
Fell over from shock.

TOHRU-KUN TOLD ME.
YES.
SO SHE REALLY IS *ALONE* THIS YEAR.

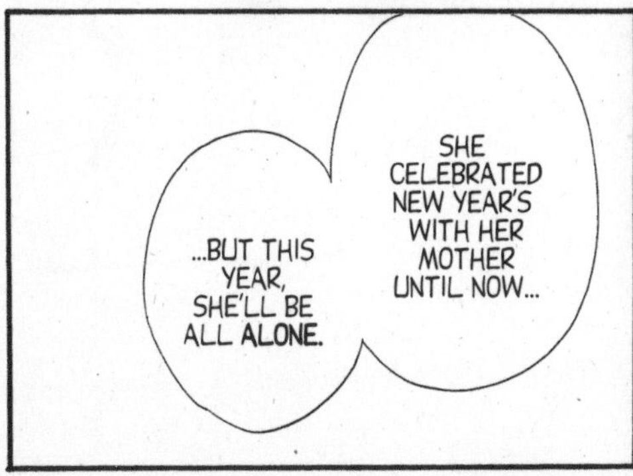

SHE CELEBRATED NEW YEAR'S WITH HER MOTHER UNTIL NOW...
...BUT THIS YEAR, SHE'LL BE ALL ALONE.

...AH!...
ARISA AND I BOTH OFFERED...
...TO SPEND IT WITH HER...
SHE JUST SMILED AND TOLD US TO SPEND IT WITH OUR FAMILIES.
BUT...
...WHAT WILL BECOME OF POOR TOHRU-KUN?

WHEN SHE SEES THE LIGHTS AND THE DECORATIONS...
...THE GOING YEAR, THE COMING YEAR...
...SHE CAN'T HELP BUT REMEMBER SEEING THEM WITH HER MOTHER.
I WONDER HOW SHE'LL FEEL?
BACK THEN...
...HOW DID SHE FEEL...
...WHEN SHE WATCHED US LEAVE?
WAS TOHRU-KUN ...
...REALLY OKAY WITH THAT?
IS SHE...
...GOING TO BE ALL RIGHT?

HOW DOES SHE FEEL...
...RIGHT NOW...
...ALONE IN THAT HOUSE?
......!
WHAT ARE YOU TWO DOING?
I saw it...
WHAT'S WITH YOU?!
I THOUGHT YOU WERE IN A HURRY TO SEE YOUR BELOVED AKITO!
When he tried stand up, Kyo Sohma's head...
WHAT ABOUT YOU?! WOULDN'T WANT TO KEEP YOUR DARLING KAGURA WAITING.
...crashed into Yuki Sohma's cheek (the lower part) as Yuki tried to go forward.
Gimme a break!
WHY DON'T I WRAP HER UP AND GIVE HER TO YOU!
AND I'LL GIVE YOU AKITO.
I DON'T WANT 'IM!
HEY, YOU TWO, WHERE ARE YOU GOING?
End of explanation.

WE'RE GOING HOME!
ズンズンズンズンズン
ぎゃあ
ぎゃあ
ぎゃあ
ぎゃあ
ぎゃあ
ぎゃあ
......
SAKI-CHAN...
...DID YOU PLAN THAT?
I DON'T CARE...
...WHAT THEY DO.
I SIMPLY WANTED TO DO SOMETHING FOR TOHRU-KUN... THAT IS ALL.

MAY YOU HAVE...
...GOOD WAVES NEXT YEAR.
IT'S BEEN FOUR MONTHS SINCE WE STARTED LIVING TOGETHER...
...BUT THERE'S STILL SOMETHING I HAVEN'T GRASPED.
She's good...
ポリポリ

I LET IT SLIP BY ME.
I NEVER REALIZED...
...BECAUSE SHE'S ALWAYS SMILING SO PLEASANT-LY.

SHE SMILES...
...AT EVEN THE SMALLEST THINGS.
YES. SHE'S ALWAYS SMILING.
AND THEN SHE TELLS ME...
...WHAT I MOST WANT TO HEAR.

WHY DIDN'T I REALIZE?
HOW COULD I MISS THAT?
I WANT TO GO HOME.
SO AT PEACE, ALL BY HERSELF...
NEW YEAR'S GIFT
I WANT TO GO HOME RIGHT NOW.
NO ONE'S LIKE THAT.

I WANT TO SEE HER.

EH...
...EEHH?!
Y-YOU STARTLED ME!
WHAT ON EARTH...
!
AH! NO! I'M NOT!
THAT IS... UM... WHAT SHOULD I SAY?!
IT ISN'T RIGHT... ME GETTING...
...ALL EMOTIONAL ON NEW YEAR'S. UM...
I WAS, UH, JUST LISTENING TO AN OLD FOLK SONG, AND MY HUMBLE JAPANESE HEART...
Oh my! Oh my!
THANK GOODNESS.

IF WE HADN'T REALIZED...
...WE WOULD HAVE...
...LEFT HER TO CRY ALL ALONE.
A-A-ARE YOU OKAY?!
WE'RE FINE.
WE JUST WANTED TO SEE... THE FIRST SUNRISE.
BUT NOT BEFORE WE EAT NEW YEAR'S SOBA.
は
×2
HUUHH ?!

I'M
HOME!

I'M HOME.
WELCOME BACK.
WELCOME BACK, SHIGURE-SAN.
YOU'RE LATE.
YOU'RE THE LAST ONE HERE.
HEY, HAA-KUN, THANKS FOR COMING TO GREET ME.
Long time no see.
...WHERE ARE KYO AND YUKI?
UMM, HOW SHALL I PUT THIS?
WELL, TO BE BLUNT...
THEY DITCHED.

...OH.
I CAN JUST IMAGINE KAGURA, RAGING LIKE FIRE...
...AND AKITO, QUIETLY STEAMING...
WHAT ARE YOU GOING TO DO, SENSEI?
I'LL TAKE CARE OF AKITO-SAN.
MAN...AND HERE I WAS PLANNING TO CHALLENGE HIM TO ONE LAST FIGHT FOR THE YEAR.
I GUESS I'LL HAVE TO TAKE IT TO HIM IN THE NEW YEAR.
Haa-kun, don't destroy my house...
BUT I DO UNDERSTAND WHY THEY'D WANT TO SKIP OUT...
EVEN I HAVE THINGS I CAN'T STAND.
AND SOMETIMES EVEN I WANT TO RUN AWAY...

NO, NO, THIS YEAR, I DON'T THINK...
...IT'S BECAUSE THEY'RE TRYING TO RUN AWAY.
?
WHAT DO YOU MEAN?
SHII-CHAN! HARUUU!
YOU FINALLY MADE IT!
THE BANQUET IS STARTING!
HEY, MOMIJI!
I'M LOOKING FORWARD TO YOUR DANCE.
Ja!
...BUT BEFORE THAT-- AKITO.
I WONDER HOW HE'LL TAKE THE NEWS.
....

THAT'S RIGHT.

GOOD EVENING.

FOR NOW...

...YOU'RE PATHETIC...

...AKITO.

EH?

HANA-CHAN?

YEAH. WE MET HER ON THE WAY THERE.

HANA-CHAN...
YOU'RE THE FIRST PERSON I'M GOING TO CALL THIS YEAR!
I'll be waiting...
Ah!
UM...BUT IS IT REALLY OKAY WITH THE SOHMA FAMILY?
I'M NOT CAUSING TROUBLE...BY BEING THE ONLY HAPPY ONE, AM I?
IT'S FINE. WE'LL GO WISH THEM HAPPY NEW YEAR DURING SANGA-NICHI.
MAYBE.

O...OKAY.
RIGHT ABOUT NOW...
...THEY'RE PROBABLY IN THE MIDDLE OF THE BANQUET.

BUT I FEEL STRANGELY RELIEVED.
I DON'T FEEL AN OUNCE OF GUILT.
I WONDER IF AKITO'S MAD.

THIS TIME...
...I'VE CONSIDERED EVERYTHING...
...I'VE THOUGHT THINGS OVER...

... ABOUT HOW I REALLY FEEL...
HAVE YOU DECIDED WHAT TO WISH FOR?
LOOK!
THE SUN'S COMING UP!
I KNOW MY WISH!
...AND WHAT I REALLY WANTED.

AND I THINK IT JUST MIGHT BE...

...TO GREET THE NEW YEAR WITH HER.

This year I'm going to beat that damn rat!

Yeah, yeah. Keep wishing.

Happy New Year!

Chapter 12

"HATORI IS LIKE SNOW."
FOR A LONG TIME, IF AKITO OR MY FATHER...
...ORDERED ME TO DO IT...I WOULD SUPPRESS ANYONE'S MEMORIES.
SO EVEN THOUGH I KNEW IT WOULD HURT YUKI...
...WHEN AKITO UTTERED THOSE WORDS...
...I ERASED HIS FRIENDS' MEMORIES.
THAT'S WHY...
"HE'S COLD LIKE SNOW."

ULTRA SPECIAL BLAH BLAH BLAH 6

Starting in this chapter, Hatori's hair is longer...I'm sure Akito told him not to cut it...I don't think Hatori will meet Kana after this. Even if Hatori could meet her again, I don't think he'd want to.

...IN A WAY, HE WAS TELLING THE TRUTH.
HATORI-SAN!
huff
THANK GOODNESS...
...IT REALLY *IS* YOU, HATORI-SAN!
huff huff
I WAS WONDERING WHAT I'D DO IF YOU WEREN'T!
TOHRU... HONDA?
huff huff
HAPPY NEW YEAR.
Suddenly brought back to reality. He's kind of out of it.
HAPPY NEW YEAR.
FOR A SECOND, I DIDN'T KNOW WHO YOU WERE.
You grew your hair longer.

IT LOOKS REALLY GOOD.
JUST LIKE SHIGURE-SAN'S.

WHAT ...?

...I'VE JUST BEEN BUSY WITH THE NEW YEAR.
I DID THINK OF GETTING IT CUT.
MAYBE...
...HE DOESN'T LIKE IT?

ARE YOU ALONE?
YES!
I WAS JUST WITH MY FRIENDS ON OUR FIRST TEMPLE VISIT OF THE NEW YEAR.

SOHMA-KUN AND KYO-KUN SAID THEY'D GO TO THE MAIN HOUSE TO WISH EVERYONE A HAPPY NEW YEAR!

THEY MUST HAVE BEEN LYING.
No doubt they're now sitting under a kotatsu eating oranges or something...
NEVER MIND KYO, YUKI'S SHOWING A LOT OF GUTS.
HE CREATED QUITE A STIR...THIS IS THE FIRST TIME THE RAT'S SKIPPED OUT ON THE BANQUET.

HOW-EVER...
"I'M SURE HE WANTED TO GREET THE NEW YEAR WITH TOHRU-KUN."
WHO COULD BLAME HIM...
HATORI-SAN, ARE YOU GOING SHOPPING?
NO...I JUST WANTED A LITTLE CITY AIR.
YOU MUST HAVE BEEN REALLY BUSY.
...FOR CHOOSING HER...
AH!
...OVER AKITO?
IT'S SNOWING...
TODAY'S GOING TO BE A COLD ONE.
Hee Hee!
SOMEHOW...
...IT'S STRANGE THAT I'M SEEING THE FIRST SNOW WITH YOU, HATORI-SAN.
I KNOW...

...I COULDN'T.
HYAH?!
!
......AH!

Fruits Basket 2 Part 6:

I usually don't have a clear idea of characters' voices, and when I do, it's rare. I say that, but even from Chapter 1, I imagined Midorikawa-san's voice for Raimon in my head. I also imagined his voice for Tamaki in Gen'ei Muso...(laugh). I never thought I would hear it in real life...! <sob> (sparkle) As for Furuba...well, I think I've daydreamed enough and need to tell myself to wake up. Sorry... (There aren't any plans to.) But, but! Kouda-san as Kotobuki is explosively adorable! (More than the original Kotobuki.) Midorikawa-san as Raimon is wow...! Ok, I need to calm down... And Shouka and Yu and Hare and Rokuro and Addy and Yan and Fear and Tooya and Hilt fit the images perfectly, so I'm really happy!! I really, really want people to hear it! I'll be even more happy if people tell me they liked it. Thank you to all the voice-over actors who took time out of their busy schedules to be on this CD!

WATER RRRR!
S-SEA WATER?!
OR FRESH WATER?!
Height: 8cm
WHICH IS IT, HATORI-SAAAN?!
...YES.
MY FRIENDS LAUGHED AT ME ABOUT IT...
HOW COME HAA-SAN IS THE ONLY WEIRD ONE?
IT COULDN'T BE ANY FUNNIER IF HE TURNED INTO A REAL DRAGON.
YOU'RE THE YEAR OF THE DRAGON, SO YOU MUST BE THE DRAGON'S BASTARD OFFSPRING!
THIS BRINGS BACK MEMORIES. TOHRU HONDA'S REACTION IS THE SAME AS HERS WAS.

HERS...
KANA'S.
PLEASED TO MEET YOU. I'M KANA SOHMA!
I WILL DO MY BEST TO ASSIST YOU!
YOU KNOW... IT'S STRANGE. WE'RE PART OF THE SAME FAMILY, YET WE HAVEN'T SPOKEN BEFORE TODAY.
I KNOW IT'S SUDDEN, BUT I HAVE A JOB FOR YOU...
Ah!
AH! IT'S SNOWING! I KNEW IT WAS GOING TO SNOW!
HATORI-SAN, EVERYONE THINKS YOU'RE SO HAND-SOME, YOU'RE POPULAR EVEN "OUTSIDE."
......
Oh yeah!
MAY I ASK YOU A QUESTION?
WHEN SNOW MELTS, WHAT DOES IT BECOME?!

IS SHE MAKING FUN OF ME?
IT BECOMES WATER, OF COURSE.
WRONG!
IT BECOMES SPRING!
SPRING IS MY FAVORITE SEASON!
THEY SAY THAT...
...BEING WITH ANOTHER PERSON...
...CAN MAKE YOU FEEL SO MUCH MORE ALIVE.
I REALIZED THEN WHAT PEOPLE THOSE MEANT.

TO ME...
...SHE WAS SPRING.
IT WAS AS IF WHILE IMPRISONED INSIDE THE DARK CAGE OF THE INNER FAMILY...
...I HAD COMPLETELY FROZEN INTO SNOW...
...AND THEN THERE SHE WAS--FRESH, CLEAR SPRING.
IT WAS ALMOST INEVITABLE THAT...
...I WOULD FALL IN LOVE WITH HER.

BUT IT WAS ALSO INEVIT-ABLE...
...THAT SHE WOULD FIND OUT.
WAAA-TERRR!
OR SEA WATER?! WHICH IS IT?!
And he really is 8cm tall.
WHICH IS IT, HATORI?!
......
IT'S A LITTLE LATE NOW...
...BUT IF YOU THREW A REAL SEA HORSE INTO A BATHTUB, IT WOULD DIE.
Probably.
YOU THINK SO...?
Y-
SORRY. I PANICKED. I DID THE FIRST THING THAT CAME TO ME.

IT ALL MAKES SENSE NOW.
I WAS WONDERING WHY YOU WOULD NEVER HOLD ME.
I UNDER-STAND.
YOU MUST HAVE BEEN SCARED.
YOU DIDN'T WANT ANYONE TO KNOW YOUR SECRET.
NATURALLY, YOU WOULD DISTANCE YOURSELF FROM OTHERS.
ESPECIALLY IF...
...IT WAS SOMEONE YOU LOVED.
BUT...
...THERE'S NO NEED TO BE SCARED ANYMORE.
DON'T PUSH ME AWAY.
I'M...HAPPY I MET YOU, HATORI.

I'M HAPPY THAT...
...I FELL IN LOVE WITH YOU.
I *WANT* TO BE NEAR YOU.
I STARTED CRYING.
IT WAS THE FIRST TIME IN MY LIFE THAT I FELT FORGIVEN.
LIKE I WAS SAVED.
LIKE THE FROZEN SNOW THAT'S MELTED BY THE BREATH OF SPRING...
...THE TEARS WOULDN'T STOP.

THE NEXT TWO MONTHS WERE LITERALLY...
...LIKE A DREAM.
"IT'S AS IF A LIFE-TIME OF HAPPINESS HAS BEEN CONDENSED INTO TWO SHORT MONTHS!"...
...SHE SAID, SMILING.
NOW, THAT SMILE PIERCES MY HEART.
THE END OF THE DREAM...
...CAME WHEN I WENT TO ASK AKITO FOR HIS PERMISSION...
...TO MARRY HER.
AKITO!
HOLD ON A SECOND! CALM DOWN... STOP!

WHY WOULD ...
KANA-CHAN, HURRY! HELP HATORI...
WHY WOULD I GIVE HIM TO YOU?! I DON'T NEED YOU!
YOU CAN'T EVEN BREAK THE CURSE! I DON'T NEED YOU! I DON'T! I DON'T!
AKITO!
IF HATORI GOES BLIND, IT'S YOUR FAULT!
IT'S YOUR FAULT! IT'S YOUR FAULT! IT'S YOUR FAULT!
IT'S YOUR FAULT...!

NO MATTER WHAT I SAID OR DID...

...SHE DID NOTHING BUT CRY.

I COULDN'T EVEN BLAME AKITO.

IT WAS THE *CURSE*.

AND SO, SHE FELL ILL

...SHE FELL ILL.

HER HEART FELL ILL.

YOUR MEMORY SUPPRESSION SKILLS WOULD BE HELPFUL NOW, WOULDN'T THEY?

JUST ERASE HER MEMORIES.

YOU HAD NO PROBLEM WITH THE *OTHERS*.

WHAT'S HURTING HER RIGHT NOW IS HER MEMORIES OF *YOU.*
HER *LOVE* FOR YOU.
ISN'T IT YOUR FINAL DUTY TO *FREE* HER FROM THAT PAIN?
I THINK SHE TRULY WANTS TO BE RELEASED.
SHE *WANTS...*
...TO FORGET.
I THINK IT WOULD HAVE BEEN BETTER...
...IF WE'D NEVER MET...
I THINK...

"SHE WANTS TO FORGET."
IT WOULD HAVE BEEN BETTER...
...IF WE'D NEVER MET...
EVEN THOUGH IT HURT PEOPLE, AND MADE THEM CRY...
...IF IT WAS AN ORDER, I WOULD PEEL AWAY PEOPLE'S MEMORIES, WITHOUT REMORSE.
IS THIS MY PUNISH-MENT?
IS THIS ...
I NEVER THOUGHT I'D HAVE TO ERASE WITH MY OWN HANDS...
...THE MEMORIES OF THE ONE PERSON MOST IMPORTANT TO ME...
...THE MEMORIES MOST IMPORTANT TO ME.
... RETRI-BUTION ?

I COULDN'T...
PRO...
...TECT... YOU...
......
...RY...
I'M SORRY...
...I'M SO SORRY.
I'M SO SORRY!
HATORI...
...I'M...

...HAPPY I MET YOU, HATORI.
NO. I'M THE ONE ...
...WHO SHOULD APOLOGIZE.

I'M THE ONE WHO COULDN'T PROTECT YOU.

BUT DESPITE THAT, YOU THOUGHT ONLY OF ME TILL THE VERY END.

IF THAT IS THE DEPTH OF HER LOVE...

...IF THAT WAS WHY SHE BECAME SO SICK...

...THEN IT'S NOT RIGHT FOR HER TO SUFFER.

THANK YOU...

...KANA...

IT'S ...

...ALL RIGHT NOW.

THERE'S ...
...NOTHING THERE TO HURT ANYMORE.
OH, GOD...
...PLEASE LET HER...
...FIND SOMEONE WHO CAN MAKE HER HAPPY.
I PRAY.
EVEN IF I DIE SURROUNDED BY SNOW THAT NEVER MELTS...
...I DON'T CARE.

PLEASE...

PLEASE...

HATORI-SAN!

HATORI-SAN...

HATORI-SAN!
......
I'M COLD.
TH-THAT'S BECAUSE... UNDER THE COAT...
Um...
... you're naked...
AH! NO, I DIDN'T SEE ANYTHING!
DO YOU REMEMBER? YOU MET ME, AND I FELL, AND...
...YOU HIT YOUR HEAD AND TRANSFORMED!
DID YOU SEE?
No! I didn't!
MY... ZODIAC...
OH...
THAT'S RIGHT.
I didn't know what to do, so I moved you somewhere where no one would see.
And then you changed back, but I didn't--!
Ah...
...YES.

Self-conscious

BU–

BUT I DON'T THINK IT'S FUNNY OR ANYTHING.

I WAS SURPRISED, BUT YOU WERE SO CUTE, AND I NEVER EXPECTED...

IT'S BEEN A LONG TIME...

...SINCE I'VE DREAMT OF KANA.

...I'M GOING TO GET DRESSED, NOW.

OH!

I'LL GO GET YOU SOMETHING WARM TO DRINK!

SO... WHY NOW?

I WONDER IF IT'S THE SNOW.

REALLY? FINALLY!

CONGRATU-LATIONS, KANA!

WE WERE WONDERING WHY YOU SUDDENLY CAME BACK TO TOKYO.

NEXT YOU'LL BE TALKING TO YOUR PARENTS ABOUT THE CEREMONY, RIGHT?

WHY DIDN'T YOU BRING YOUR FIANCÉ?

I wanted to meet him!

WELL, HE'S BUSY WITH WORK.
AND WE'RE HAVING THE CEREMONY IN HIS TOWN.
HEY, WHAT KIND OF GUY IS HE?
THE KIND WHO CAN'T LIE.
AND I FEEL SO CALM WHEN I'M WITH HIM.
EVEN IF...
...HE'S NOT AS GOOD-LOOKING AS HATORI-SAN.
Oohh, look what you're saying!
WELL, I WAS ALWAYS IN LOVE WITH HIM.
BUT IT WAS JUST ONE-SIDED.
THIS IS THE FIRST TIME I'VE BEEN BACK TO THE SOHMA HOUSE IN A LONG TIME...
I WONDER IF I'LL GET TO SEE HATORI-SAN?

JUST DON'T HAVE AN AFFAIR!
I WON'T! NYAH.
I'M MADLY IN LOVE!
I HADN'T SEEN HER IN TWO YEARS.
SHE WAS SMILING THE SAME WAY SHE DID BACK THEN.
I SEE. SO SHE'S ...
... HAPPY NOW.
I'M GLAD.
I'M GLAD...
... CONGRATU-LATIONS.

CONGRATULATIONS... ON WHAT?

NO...

IT'S NOTHING.

TIME PASSES SLOWLY...

?

...BUT STEADILY.

I WOULD BE LYING IF I SAID THAT I WASN'T SHOCKED...

...BUT I'M HAPPY...

...TO KNOW THAT IT WAS A GOOD THING... TO I LET HER GO.

I'M GLAD.

"PLEASE, LET HER BE HAPPY.
EVEN IF I DIE SURROUNDED BY SNOW...
...THAT NEVER MELTS."
"HATORI-SAN...

...WHEN SNOW MELTS, WHAT DOES IT BECOME?"
...SNOW MELTS, WHAT DO YOU THINK IT BECOMES?
HUH?
......
WHEN ...
AH...UM, WELL... HMM.
IT BECOMES SPRING!
NO MATTER HOW COLD IT IS NOW...
IT'S STRANGE, ISN'T IT? BUT IT'S TRUE.
...SPRING WILL COME AGAIN!
WITHOUT FAIL.

SOMEDAY...
...THE SNOW WILL MELT.
NO MATTER HOW COLD IT IS NOW...
Is coffee okay?
Here's your bag.
WITHOUT FAIL.
WITHOUT FAIL.
To be continued in Volume 3...

Next time in...

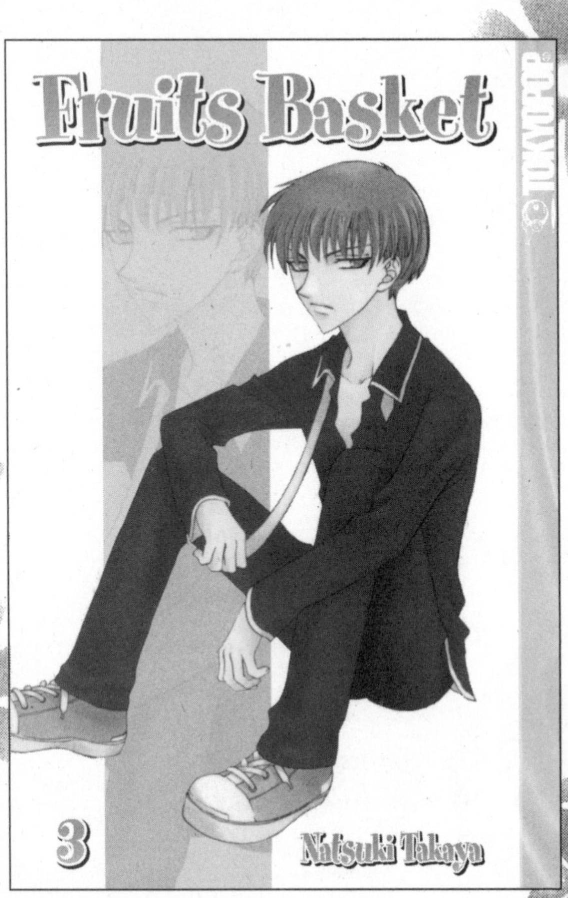

Hot Springs and Cold Feet

It's Valentines Day and you know what that means—lots of chocolates for the cutest boys at school! But who will score the most-- hotheaded Kyo or "prince charming" Yuki? Of course the kind-hearted Tohru, guest of the Sohma family, has chocolates for everyone! But when White Day comes around, what will the Sohma family give back?

Fruits Basket Volume 3
Available Now

How to Play Rich Man, Poor Man
(Dai Hin Min / Dai Fugo)

OBJECTIVE
The aim is to get rid of all your cards as soon as possible.

PLAYERS AND CARDS
About 4 to 7 people using a standard 54 card pack with jokers. The suits are irrelevant and the cards rank, from high to low with deuces high: 2 A K Q J 10 9 8 7 6 5 4 3. Jokers are wild.

DEAL
The game is played clockwise. All the cards are dealt out. Some players may have one more than others.

PLAY
The player to dealer's left starts by leading (face up) any single card or any set of cards of equal rank (for example, three fives). Each player in turn must then either pass (i.e. not play any cards), or play face up a card or set of cards which beats the previous play.

A single card is beaten by any higher single card. A set of cards can only be beaten by a higher set containing the same number of cards. So for example, if the previous player played two sixes, you can beat this with two kings, or two sevens, but not with a single king, and not with three sevens (though you could play two of them and hang onto the third).

It is not necessary to beat the previous play just because you can -- passing is always allowed. Also passing does not prevent you from playing the next time your turn comes round.

The play continues as many times around the table as necessary until someone makes a play which everyone else passes. All the cards played are then turned face down and put to one side, and the player who played last (and highest) in the previous "trick" starts again by leading any card or set of equal cards.

For example the play might go:
Tohru leads with a pair of fours. Kyo follows with a pair of sevens. Uo passes. Hanajima follows with a pair of Tens. Tohru passes. Kyo plays a pair of Jacks. Uo passes. Hanajima passes. Tohru passes. Kyo then starts again by leading any card or set.

When a player whose turn it is to play has no more cards left, the turn passes to the next player in rotation. Therefore in the example, if the two Jacks were Kyo's last two cards, he would sit out the rest of the round and it would then be Uo's turn to play anything.

Jokers are wild and are equal in rank to whatever card they are played with.

For scoring purposes, whoever goes out first gets 2 points, second out gets one point and the rest of the players get no points.

SOCIAL STATUS
The first player who is out of cards is dubbed the "Dai Fugo," or very rich man. Other variations on the rules call this person the President, King, or the Great Dalmuti. The last player to be left with any cards is known as the "Dai Hin Min," or very poor man. You can also use other derisive terms such as peon, beggar, scum, or a--hole.

While it's not part of the basic Dai Hin Min rules, many variations also give titles to the players based on their rank. So if you use "King" as your model, you might have King, Duke, Knight, Merchant, and Peon as your ranks. More importantly, the players of higher status are entitled to enjoy and generally abuse their power over the lower ranking players. You can also add to the fun by having players wear hats based on rank, with the leader wearing a crown and the loser wearing a dunce cap.

Between hands, players move seats based on ranks. The Dai Fugo selects the most comfortable chair; second place sits to the left, and so on around to the Dai Hin Min who sits to the Dai Fugo's right, probably on a crate or packing case.

The Dai Hin Min is responsible for shuffling, dealing and clearing away the cards when necessary. As the players are now seated clockwise in order of rank, the first card is dealt to the Dai Fugo, and so on down.

When the deal is complete, the Dai Hin Min must give his or her highest card to the Dai Fugo, and the Dai Fugo gives back in exchange any card that he or she does not want. Second place trades with second from last, etc. If there are an odd number of players, the middle player doesn't swap. (Variation: swap 2 cards per round)

The Dai Hin Min then leads any card or set of cards and the game continues as before.

END OF GAME
If scoring, set a target score (say 11 points). The game ends when someone reaches it.

VARIATIONS

Shibari
If a player follows a play with a card of the same suit, that player may declare "shibari," or "binding," which means that all other players must follow suit in order to play. For example, if Hanajima plays a seven of clubs and Tohru trumps it with a nine of clubs, she can declare shibari on clubs, and only clubs can be played. This variation can work with doubles and triples, too. Example—Kyo plays a six of clubs and a six of hearts. Uo trumps that with a eight of diamonds and an eight of hearts. She can declare shibari on hearts so that each subsequent play must have a heart plus any other. Double shibari or triple shibari can be declared if two or three suits match. Shibari's are only effective for the hand in which they are played.

Revolution!
If four of a kind are played, it is called a revolution. When this happens, the rank of cards is reversed. From that point on, lower values now trump higher values until there is another revolution.

Dai Fugo makes the rules!
Another fun variation is to let the Dai Fugo add an extra rule each round (or cancel an existing rule). The rules will likely make it easier for the Dai Fugo to keep winning or humiliating for the loser, but in Dai Hin Min, as in life, it's not always fair. But remember Karma—what comes around goes around, and you won't stay on top forever…

There are many other variations to Dai Hin Min and its Western equivalents, and the rules are slightly different depending on whoever you ask. For other variations, and rules on similar games, visit www.pagat.com, the web's leading resource for card games.

Year of the Rat: Behind the Whiskers

Rat

Years*: 1936, 1948, 1960, 1972, 1984, 1996, 2008, 2020, 2032
Positive Qualities: charming, imaginative, ambitious, sentimental, generous (to loved ones), frugal
Negative Qualities: hot-tempered, overly critical, prone to gossip, pack-rat
Suitable Jobs: sales, writing, publicity
Compatible With: Dragons, Monkeys, Oxen
Must Avoid: Horses (and cats)
Ruling Hours: 11 PM to 1 AM
Season: Winter
Ruling Month: December
Sign Direction: North
Fixed Element: Water
Corresponding Western Sign: Sagittarius

I'M NOT *THAT* CRITICAL.

The rat was at a disadvantage during the Zodiac race, but with his nimble abilities and smarts was able to land the coveted first place spot in the Chinese Zodiac. For people born in the year of the rat, this win spells some degree of financial freedom (if they don't marry a sheep), but their hearts will always remain true to family and friends. After all, friends are one thing that the rat can never have enough of.

Cheerful and always optimistic, Rats love living in groups and will gladly let a friend or relative crash for any amount of time, be it a night or ten years. Freeloading is not an issue because a rat can always find some kind of work that needs to be done. Even when someone swindles them, rats seldom hold a grudge. They simply just lock the bad memory away in their hearts. Keeping their loved ones close and happy is what matters most. Ironically though, rats also hold onto an exorbitant amount of trinkets and mementos from past experiences. This 'pack rat' mentality is detrimental though since rats often pick up or buy things they really never needed in the first place.

An interesting facet of the rat's personality is that they love to ask questions and have great memories, though they often single out the small nit-picky details and gloss over the other nicer points. It is a minor character flaw, but this cunning insight does tend make a person born in the rat year a particularly excellent writer.

While misfortune does not befall the rat often, whenever it does strike, a rat will have little to fear since an escape route was always carefully factored into their clever plans. Potential dangers are sized-up and quickly faced down with their fearless attitude, cool demeanor and quick wits. For the rat, perseverance is one of their keys to success. After all, no matter how fleeting success is...success is still success.

Celebrity Rats

Ben Affleck
Mandy Moore
Alice Cooper
Scarlett Johansson
Rizzo the Rat

Hm... On second thought, perhaps publicity isn't the job for me.

* Note: If you were born in January or early February, then chances are you are probably the animal of the preceding year. The only way to know for certain is to know on which day Chinese New Year's was held. For example, this year (2004) the Chinese New Year began on January 22, so the first three weeks of January were still year of the sheep.

Fans Basket

Do you want to share your love for Fruits Basket with fans around the world? "Fans Basket" is taking submissions of fan art, poetry, cosplay photos, or any other Furuaba fun you'd like to share!

How to submit:

1)Send your work via regular mail (NOT e-mail) to:

"Fans Basket"
c/o TOKYOPOP
5900 Wilshire Blvd.
Suite 2000
Los Angeles, CA 90036

2) All work should be in black and white and no larger than 8.5" x 11". (And try not to fold it too many times!)

3) Anything you send will not be returned. If you want to keep your original, it's fine to send us a copy.

4) Please include your full name, age, city and state for us to print with your work. If you'd rather us use a pen name, please include that too.

5) IMPORTANT: If you're under the age of 18, you must have your parent's permission in order for us to print your work. Any submissions without a signed note of parental consent cannot be used.

6) For full details, please check out our website.http://www.tokyopop.com/aboutus/fanart.php

Disclaimer: Anything you send to us becomes the exclusive property of TOKYOPOP Inc. and, as we said before, will not be returned to you. We will have the right to print, reproduce, distribute, or modify the artwork for use in future volumes of Fruits Basket or on the web royalty-free.

S-Girl,
Atlanta, GA

S-Girl

Kathy Schilling

And bonus art from TOKYOPOP's own Super Interns!

Chrissy Schilling

Here's a few haiku
I wrote about Fruits Basket
Print them if you can

Chinese Zodiac
Twelve there are but one left out
What of the poor cat?

Yuki or Kyo?
We don't know who Tohru picks
But I like the Rat

-Kathleen B.
West Hartford, CT

SOUND EFFECT INDEX

THE FOLLOWING IS A LIST OF THE SOUND EFFECTS USED IN FRUITS BASKET. EACH SOUND IS LABELED BY PAGE AND PANEL NUMBER, SEPARATED BY A PERIOD. THE FIRST DESCRIPTION IS THE PHONETIC READING OF THE JAPANESE, AND IS FOLLOWED BY THE EQUIVALENT ENGLISH SOUND OR A DESCRIPTION.

34.5	fura-fura: dazed
35.2	da-da-da-da-da: dash
35.3	dan: whack
36.3	dohki-dohki: badum-badum (pounding heartbeat)
37.4	jin: teary stare
42.1	zawa-zawa-zawa: chatter chatter
43.1	zawa-zawa: chatter chatter
43.3	gann: wham
43.4	mera-mera-mera: crackle crackle (burning rage)
47.3	gan: wham
47.4	zawa-zawa-zawa: chatter chatter
48.3	biku: eep!
48.4	doki-doki: badum-badum (heartbeat)
52.3a	zuruben: slip bam
53.3b	gann: wham
55.3	kiss (in german)
56.1	dah: dash
60.5	bikuu: eep!
64.2	gaa: blush
67.1	zawa-zawa: chatter chatter
72.2	gya-gya: chatter chatter
75.2	pachii: spark
75.3	fuii: turn
76.2	keke: cackle
77.2	don: bam
81.1	ninaka: shoop
81.5	piku: twitch
82.6	dota-dota: clatter-crash
83.2	gachan-tata-dota-bacha: bang-clatter-crash-bang
84.3	pah: pop
85.4	gashaa: grab
86.3a	bon: poof

9.2a	basa-basa: tumble
9.2b	gonn: bonk
10.3	doko: dump
12.4	pata-pata: pitter patter
12.5	gara: clatter
14.4	bag: Crunchies
15.2	bari-bari; pari-pari: munch crunch
17.1	dohki-dohki: badum-badum (pounding heartbeat)
17.4	gotoh: clunk
18.4	ga-gan: (shock)
19.1	kandou: impressed
19.4	pata-pata: pitter patter

DOKI-DOKI

ドッキ

ONE OF THE MOST COMMON SOUND EFFECTS IN MANGA, "DOKI-DOKI" IS THE SOUND OF A POUNDING HEARTBEAT. IT'S USED TO INDICATE A TENSE, EMOTIONAL SITUATION.

20.1	patan: close (door)
22.4	gara: clatter
22.6	don: ta-da!
24.3	gyaa-gyaa: bicker
27.2	zusa: trip
27.3	gaba: (panic)
28.3	pasa: plop
33.3a	carton: You'll drink it all day long! Maibuum Milk. There's just not enough!
33.3b	patan: close (door)
34.3	GU: SNORE
34.4	hiiiii: cringe

131.3 pu-pu-pu: (stifled laughter)
135.1 bag: Supermarket- Come on by!
136.4 pori-pori: scratch-scratch
138.2 pashii x3: fwip x 3
139.1 kashi-kashi-kashi:

ANGER MARKS

THESE LITTLE "PLUS SIGNS" ARE MEANT TO REPRESENT A THROBBING VEIN. OVER THE YEARS, THESE HAVE BECOME A VISUAL SHORTCUT IN MANGA FOR ANGER. IN THE FRUITS BASKET ANIME, SHIGURE POKES FUN AT HIS EASY GOING PERSONALITY BY HOLDING AN ANGER MARK IN FRONT OF HIS FACE TO SHOW HIS RANGE.

munch munch munch
139.6 pata: clack
141.4 don: thump
150.1 gashin: crash
150.5 zun-zun-zun-zun: stomp stomp
151.2a kya-kya-kya...: bicker bicker
151.2b zun-zun-zun-zun: stomp stomp
151.3 zun-zun-zun: stomp stomp
152.2 pori-pori: scratch-scratch
154.1 BASHIN: SLAM
156.1 HAx2: pantx2
170.2 tsuru: slip
170.5 gan: thunk
171.1a dosaa: thud
171.1b bon: poof
185.1 dosaa: thud

86.3b dotann: thump
86.5 basah: flutter
87.2 zawa-zawa: chatter chatter
87.3 zawa-zawa-zawa: chatter chatter
87.4 gyuu: clench
88.1 kiran: sparkle
89.2 go: punch
91.1 pasha: flash
92.3 gabaa: flop
97.5 pin-pon-pan: (intercom bell)
98.5 suu: fwip

ZAWA-ZAWA

THE SOUND OF A CROWD. IF YOU SEE "ZAWA"S IN A CLASSROOM, IT PROBABLY MEANS THAT CLASS HASN'T STARTED YET. EITHER THAT, OR A TEACHER CAN'T CONTROL HIS OR HER STUDENTS!

99.2 dokii: badum (heartbeat)
99.5 kirii: sparkle
100.1 dokii: badum (heartbeat)
100.2 doki-doki: badum-badum (heartbeat)
102.1 gara: clatter
104.1 dohki-dohki: badum-badum (pounding heartbeat)
104.2 dohki-dohki: badum-badum (pounding heartbeat)
105.1 kara-kara: rattle rattle
106.3 ha-ha-fu: huff-huff-pant
106.4 pata-pata: pitter patter
106.5 kara-kara: rattle rattle
107.4 hah: gasp
110.2 dokii: badum (heartbeat)
109.4 pata-pata: pitter patter
113.3 kara-kara: rattle rattle
121.3 kochi: plunk
122.1 dokii: badum (heartbeat)
122.5a "pu, bu: (stifled laughter)"
122.5b pu-pu-pu: (stifled laughter)
127.1 dokin: badum (heartbeat)
127.2 dokin: badum (heartbeat)
127.3 dokin-dokin: badum badum (heartbeat)
129.2 GU: SNORE

OT
OLDER TEEN
AGE 16+

STOP!

This is the back of the book. You wouldn't want to spoil a great ending!

This book is printed "manga-style," in the authentic Japanese right-to-left format. Since none of the artwork has been flipped or altered, readers get to experience the story just as the creator intended. You've been asking for it, so TOKYOPOP® delivered: authentic, hot-off-the-press, and far more fun!

DIRECTIONS

If this is your first time reading manga-style, here's a quick guide to help you understand how it works.

It's easy... just start in the top right panel and follow the numbers. Have fun, and look for more 100% authentic manga from TOKYOPOP®!

ALSO AVAILABLE FROM TOKYOPOP®

MANGA

.HACK//LEGEND OF THE TWILIGHT
@LARGE
ABENOBASHI: MAGICAL SHOPPING ARCADE
A.I. LOVE YOU
AI YORI AOSHI
ANGELIC LAYER
ARM OF KANNON
BABY BIRTH
BATTLE ROYALE
BATTLE VIXENS
BRAIN POWERED
BRIGADOON
B'TX
CANDIDATE FOR GODDESS, THE
CARDCAPTOR SAKURA
CARDCAPTOR SAKURA - MASTER OF THE CLOW
CHOBITS
CHRONICLES OF THE CURSED SWORD
CLAMP SCHOOL DETECTIVES
CLOVER
COMIC PARTY
CONFIDENTIAL CONFESSIONS
CORRECTOR YUI
COWBOY BEBOP
COWBOY BEBOP: SHOOTING STAR
CRAZY LOVE STORY
CRESCENT MOON
CULDCEPT
CYBORG 009
D•N•ANGEL
DEMON DIARY
DEMON ORORON, THE
DEUS VITAE
DIGIMON
DIGIMON TAMERS
DIGIMON ZERO TWO
DOLL
DRAGON HUNTER
DRAGON KNIGHTS
DRAGON VOICE
DREAM SAGA
DUKLYON: CLAMP SCHOOL DEFENDERS
EERIE QUEERIE!
ERICA SAKURAZAWA: COLLECTED WORKS
ET CETERA
ETERNITY
EVIL'S RETURN
FAERIES' LANDING
FAKE
FLCL
FORBIDDEN DANCE
FRUITS BASKET
G GUNDAM
GATEKEEPERS
GETBACKERS
GIRL GOT GAME
GRAVITATION
GTO
GUNDAM BLUE DESTINY
GUNDAM SEED ASTRAY
GUNDAM WING
GUNDAM WING: BATTLEFIELD OF PACIFISTS
GUNDAM WING: ENDLESS WALTZ
GUNDAM WING: THE LAST OUTPOST (G-UNIT)
HANDS OFF!
HAPPY MANIA
HARLEM BEAT
I.N.V.U.
IMMORTAL RAIN
INITIAL D
INSTANT TEEN: JUST ADD NUTS
ISLAND
JING: KING OF BANDITS
JING: KING OF BANDITS - TWILIGHT TALES
JULINE
KARE KANO
KILL ME, KISS ME
KINDAICHI CASE FILES, THE
KING OF HELL
KODOCHA: SANA'S STAGE
LAMENT OF THE LAMB
LEGAL DRUG
LEGEND OF CHUN HYANG, THE
LES BIJOUX
LOVE HINA
LUPIN III
LUPIN III: WORLD'S MOST WANTED
MAGIC KNIGHT RAYEARTH I
MAGIC KNIGHT RAYEARTH II
MAHOROMATIC: AUTOMATIC MAIDEN
MAN OF MANY FACES
MARMALADE BOY
MARS
MARS: HORSE WITH NO NAME
METROID
MINK
MIRACLE GIRLS
MIYUKI-CHAN IN WONDERLAND
MODEL
ONE
ONE I LOVE, THE
PARADISE KISS
PARASYTE
PASSION FRUIT
PEACH GIRL
PEACH GIRL: CHANGE OF HEART
PET SHOP OF HORRORS
PITA-TEN
PLANET LADDER
PLANETES
PRIEST

02.03.04T